CYCLISTS' ROUTE ATLAS

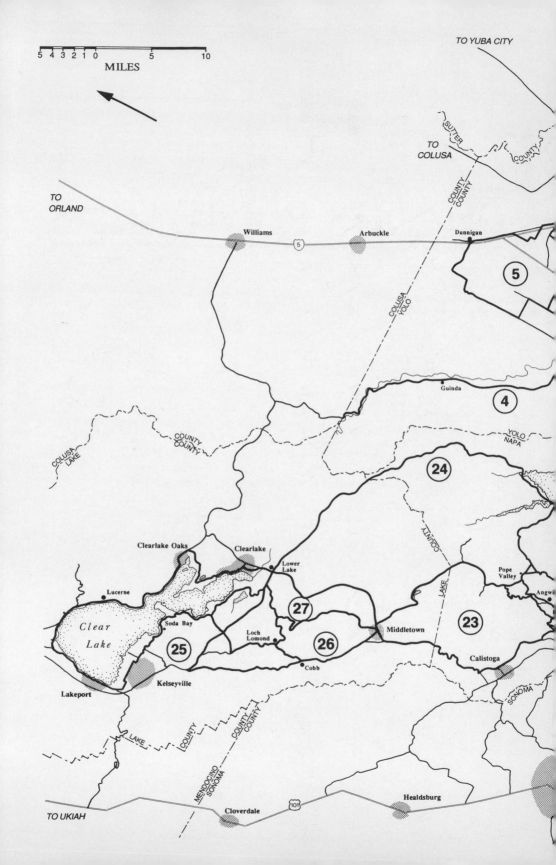

HEYDAY BOOKS

CYCLISTS' ROUTE ATLAS

A GUIDE TO

Yolo, Solano, Napa and Lake Counties

RANDALL GRAY BRAUN

Acknowledgements

　　　I would like to take this opportunity to express my gratitude to the people that have helped this book come to fruition. My parents deserve more thanks than I can ever give; they are always there in a supportive and caring way. Thanks to Valerie, the love of my life, for seeing me through all this. Thanks also to the Davis Bike Club, for providing a creative outlet; and to Helen Pool, for getting me involved when I unknowingly walked into the B&L Bike Shop in 1980. The Apple computer people need to be recognized for creating the marvelous Macintosh. (The text, the map and profile labels, and the pavement and weather charts were all created on the Macintosh and LaserWriter.) Many thanks also to Bren and Rick for sharing computer time and knowledge, and to Jeff for photographic help. And a special thank you to Heyday Books and Malcolm for giving me a second chance.

Copyright © 1986 by Randall Gray Braun

Printed in the United States of America.

10　　9　　8　　7　　6　　5　　4　　3　　2　　1

Published by Heyday Books
Box 9145
Berkeley, California 94709

ISBN: 0-930588-24-x

Cover and interior photos: Randall Braun
Cover design: Nancy Austin
Interior design and production: Randall Braun and Nancy McMichael
Editing and proofing: Rina Margolin and Estelle Jelinek

Cover photo: Solano County—Cantelow Road

For Valerie, my wife, always and always.

TABLE OF CONTENTS _____

INTRODUCTION

INTRODUCTION _____

If you enjoy cycling for the satisfaction that comes from meeting a challenge or for the lure of the open road, if you like solitude or enjoy a brisk spin with friends, close together, talking, or if being out in the wide open country under your own power refuels and refreshes you, this book is for you.

This guide, the first in a series of cyclists' route atlases' covers a four-county area in central California. The terrain varies from the flat farmlands of Yolo County to the lakes and mountains of Lake County, from the famous vineyards and back roads of Napa County to the Delta marshes and islands of Solano County. I have created twenty-seven routes, which vary in length from nine to sixty-two miles. For each route there is a written description, a map, and a topographic profile.

The purpose of this book is to provide you with high-quality route information: how far or hilly it will be, what the terrain will be like, how good the road conditions will be, and where you can get food and water along the way. With these concerns off your mind, you will be free to contemplate the scenery, the feel of the wind on your face, the sound of wheels and chain, the smells of the forest, and other equally pressing matters. The routes in this guide are not cast in stone. Use them to become familiar with the area, and then rearrange them to suit your personal requirements. If you already know this area, this guide will provide accurate reference data on your favorite roads.

After years of exploring the back roads for new hills to challenge and valleys to traverse, largely due to my involvement with the Davis Bike Club's Double Century Tour, I have come to realize that this area has some of the finest four-season cycling in California. My hope is that you too will become familiar with this area and relish all that it has to offer.

I must admit I had some hesitation in writing this guide. I remember the betrayal I felt as a boy when *Sunset* magazine did a story on a part of Northern California where our family has a summer cabin.

They described the quiet river valley where I often spent my summers. They had pictures of the rugged and desolate coast, which I loved to explore, and pictures of the sleepy little town too. They even exposed my favorite swimming hole. Fortunately, the hoards I had imagined never materialized, the people that did come also seemed to care, and the quiet little river remained the same. I now find myself in the same position as *Sunset*, with the potential to disrupt the special places of people I've never met. I am comforted by the knowledge that cyclists are a friendly, considerate bunch, who seem to be in tune with the world. I ask only that you carry this consideration with you, not just while riding in this area but wherever you go. Then I believe the people you meet will be more willing to share their special places with those of us who follow.

SAFETY

One of the goals of this guide is to promote safe cycling. Unfortunately, you can't acquire quality riding technique from a book. The knowledge you need must be acquired the old-fashioned way: you have to earn it. That means putting in the miles, trial and error, and emulating the good technique of others. Nevertheless, let me touch on a few points that I have found to be important.

* Wear a helmet; they save lives.

* Ride in a consistent, predictable manner, and obey the rules of the road, especially stop signs. By doing so, you are saying to other traffic, "You can trust me." Squirrely behavior makes other drivers and cyclists very nervous.

* Always ride within your ability to respond to the unexpected.

After a few years of cycling, your ability to read the road will become sharper. But the tight corner you forgot about or the gravel that wasn't there last time can result in serious injury.

* On narrow roads and on fast descents, claim your space out from the right shoulder. The danger comes when a passing vehicle is forced to choose between hitting an oncoming vehicle or running you off the road. When a vehicle approaches from behind and you can see the road ahead is clear, move over and allow it to pass. It is also important to deal with these situations in a courteous manner and not be a lout.

* Never assume anything. Statements like "I thought he saw me" or "I thought I could make it" are often said in the hospital.

* Keep your machine in top condition. Functional brakes and gears can come in handy.

Cycling is an exhilarating, healthy, and safe means of transportation and recreation. If you practice good habits whenever you ride, cycling can enrich your life well into your golden years.

AVERAGE PAVEMENT QUALITY

Pavement quality is important to cycling. Riding miles of bumpy pavement, dodging open potholes, and slowing for gravel detract from the enjoyment of any bike route. The rating system I have devised is easy to understand. All pavements are divided into four grades, which are then averaged over the length of each route. Thus, if a given route is half Grade One and half Grade Two, its Average Pavement Quality would be 1.5. An A.P.Q. rating is given at the beginning of each route description. A detailed pavement quality summary is given in the appendix.

GRADE ONE: This is smooth, even, usually new pavement, technically called asphalt. It is free of cracks, patches, and loose surface material. For roller skating, Grade One would be preferable. For cycling, its smooth surface offers little rolling resistance; thus, you don't fatigue as quickly. Most urban streets and expressways are Grade One.

GRADE TWO: Coarse yet even-textured pavement, technically called "chip seal," characterizes Grade Two. Chip seal is a crushed gravel product, like Rice Crispies, often applied over cracked or broken asphalt to increase its life span. It is usually free of surface irregularities, but occasional cracks and patches are to be expected. Although it offers more rolling resistance than Grade One, the large wheel diameters of a bicycle make for a pleasant ride. One nice aspect of Grade Two is the more use it gets, the smoother it becomes. Most of the rural roads in Yolo County are Grade Two.

GRADE THREE: Patched, broken, bumpy pavement with occasional open potholes and cracks qualifies as Grade Three. The surface texture is irregular and commonly worn and rutted from many years of use. Grade Three is usually found on lightly-traveled roads where weather damage has been repeatedly repaired. There are no long stretches of Grade Three in any of these routes. Ascending a Grade Three slope is preferable to descending it because of the reduced speed.

GRADE FOUR: These are gravel-covered dirt roads or roads with badly broken pavement and large amounts of surface debris. On medium-use roads, Grade Four is usually a temporary feature, waiting for the weather to dry up or the county budget to flow. Roads in central Solano and northern Lake counties are almost entirely gravel-covered. However, the routes presented in this guide bypass the Grade Four roads in these areas.

In addition to their beautiful, exciting, scenic, warm, serene, challenging, peaceful year-round appeal, the roads in this area have remarkably high pavement quality. Of the 1,121 miles of routes presented, only 21.5 miles are Grade Three and a mere 1.5 miles are Grade Four. That's 98% Grade One and Grade Two pavement!

TOTAL CLIMB

    This number appearing at the beginning of each route description represents the total feet climbed. The elevation data was obtained with an aircraft altimeter during the route-measuring process. To decide how challenging a route might be, you must also consider total distance, duration of each climb, and the rate of the climb. For example, ROUTE #27 climbs 3,500 feet in 57.5 miles, or sixty-one feet per mile. This may seem like a lot, but ROUTE #20 climbs over 2,000 feet in just 10.3 miles, or 194 feet per mile!

    Most of the routes presented are loops, so the T.C. figure would be the same no matter in which direction you travel. One-way routes such as ROUTE #4, Cache Creek Express, would have different totals if measured in the other direction.

    Most of the climbs in this guide are, in my opinion, well within the ability of the average cyclist. It would totally defeat the purpose of this book if any of the climbing data prevents you from enjoying these hills and valleys. If you haven't already, you will soon discover that the more you ride, the smaller the hills become. So remember, what seems insurmountable today will be challenging tomorrow, and what is a challenge tomorrow will be an achievement next weekend.

MAP KEY

✪	START/FINISH POINT (SERVICES)	(shaded circle)	LARGE CITY, TOWN (SERVICES)
✪	START/FINISH POINT (NO SERVICES)	=⊏	FREEWAY WITH OVERPASS
★	TURN AROUND POINT	◯◖	STATE, INTERSTATE HIGHWAY
●●•	CITY, TOWN, STORE (SERVICES)	······	FERRY CROSSING
◯	TOWN (NO SERVICES)	– – –	COUNTY LINE
▲	CAMPING	⊢⊢⊢⊢⊢⊢	RAILROAD TRACKS
——	MAIN ROUTE	(creek icon)	CREEK, LAKE, DAM
——	CONNECTING ROAD	(textured box)	PARK, FOREST
– – – –	BIKE PATH	(marsh icon)	MARSHLANDS
☐→	ROUTE DIRECTION	(gravel icon)	GRAVEL AREA

YOLO COUNTY

YOLO COUNTY
INTRODUCTION

Yolo County has been my home for the last five years, and cycling these roads remains a challenge and a joy. Contrary to some people's opinions, this is not boring cycling country, because hills are not a requirement for enjoyable cycling. Don't get me wrong; I like hills. Some of my best friends are hills. This county just doesn't have very many. What this area does have is solitude, open space, quiet, and lots of room to roam.

There are two major population centers in Yolo County, Woodland and Davis. Woodland, the county seat, is oriented toward agricultural industry, while Davis is oriented toward the University of California with its large student population. Both are growing, vibrant communities, whereas other towns in the county, such as Knights Landing and Esparto, seem to have constant or slowly declining populations.

Yolo County is largely flat agricultural land, where the fields come right up to the road. It is the largest producer of processed tomatoes in the United States, with loaded trucks racing from field to factory a common sight throughout the summer. Corn, wheat, and rice are also typical crops here, each adding a different texture to the area. Because of all the agricultural activity, hard-working farmers and their equipment travel these roads seven days a week. As enjoyable as it is to cycle down the middle of a deserted road, it takes only a little effort to be aware of other vehicles and move to the right as they approach. Experience has shown me that if I am courteous toward the farmers, they are more than willing to return the favor.

The regions surrounding Esparto and up into the Capay Valley have been producing almonds for many years. Almonds flower in the spring, and as long as you're not allergic to the blossoms, this is the nicest time to ride among the orchards. Cache Creek, in the northwestern corner of the county, is a good-sized river from late spring into summer, with rafting, "tubing," and camping all popular activities.

Actually there are "hills" in Yolo County, but some cyclists still prefer to call it wind. The most common year-round wind direction is out of the northwest, coming down the Sacramento Valley. It is both fun and challenging to "climb the hill" up to Esparto or Knights Landing, then sail almost effortlessly back to Davis.

Winter fog is not uncommon in the Central Valley and can be a hazard to cyclists, but it forms less often in Yolo than in Sacramento County. Other hazards one might encounter are crop dusting, usually done in the very early morning hours, and agricultural burning, often lasting a few weeks in the fall. Heat and sunburn are hazards no matter where you ride in the summer months, so be sure to take adequate precautions, drink plenty of water, and use sun screen--or refrain from riding in the afternoon heat. For those of you not living in Davis and wishing to ride the routes starting there, I recommend beginning at the shopping centers, a half mile east of both Davis starting points shown on the maps.

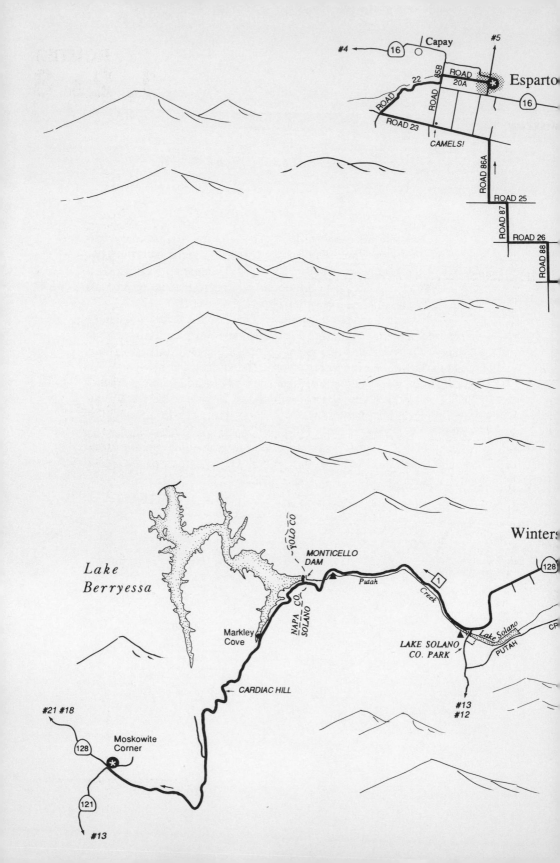

ROUTES
1, 2 & 3

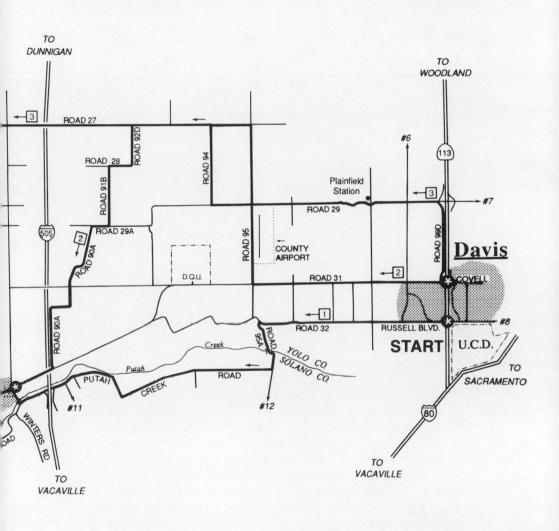

TO
WOODLAND

TO
DUNNIGAN

TO
WOODLAND

3 ROAD 27

ROAD 92D

ROAD 28

ROAD 94

ROAD 91B

113

Plainfield
Station

ROAD 29

3

#6

#7

505

2

ROAD 29A

ROAD 90A

ROAD 95

COUNTY
AIRPORT

ROAD 99D

Davis

D.Q.U.

ROAD 31

2

COVELL

1

ROAD 32

RUSSELL BLVD.

#8

ROAD 90A

Creek

95A

ROAD

YOLO CO.

SOLANO CO.

START

U.C.D.

TO
SACRAMENTO

Putah

PUTAH

CREEK

ROAD

#11

#12

WINTERS RD.

80

OAD

TO
VACAVILLE

TO
VACAVILLE

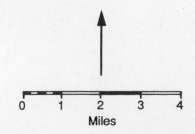

0   1   2   3   4
Miles

1 OUT TO CARDIAC _____

Starting Point: *Davis*
Distance: *33.8 miles one way*
Total Climb: *1,530 ft.*

Average Pavement Quality: *1.5*
Map: *Pages 12-13*

No matter what their ability, riding "out to Cardiac" is a year-round favorite of Davis cyclists. Rain or shine, eight days a week, you will find somebody out there riding. "Ironman" Dave Scott can often be found on his favorite training ride, hammering up Cardiac Hill or flying back down in a blur.

Start on Russell Boulevard at the Highway 113 overpass. Head west on Russell Blvd. or use the bike path that parallels it. The path ends **4.8** miles later at Road 95A where you turn south. You enter Solano County as you cross the double-arched Stevenson Bridge, now a popular place for high school kids to proclaim their true love using spray paint. Take the next turn west onto Putah Creek Road and travel by walnut and almond groves, past lines of olive trees, and beside open fields of corn, beans, tomatoes, and alfalfa. At Winters Road turn north across the bridge and into Winters where there is a grocery and a bike shop on Main Street. More services (food, restrooms) are available as you turn west on Grant Street, which is also Highway 128. Just a half mile further west there's a great fruit stand that specializes in dried fruit; their dried pears are absolutely heavenly.

The traffic increases but the shoulder is wide until Lake Solano Park (see ROUTE #13) with water and restrooms there. As you enter the cool canyon below Lake Berryessa, the road narrows and can be quite busy on summer weekends with the "gotta go to the lake" traffic, so be alert. Just beyond the American Trails store and campground at mile **22.5**, begin the short, sweet climb up to Monticello Dam and enter Napa County. The real climb, the purpose of your journey, begins as you pass Markley Cove Store--Cardiac Hill. I am sure Cardiac was named by a cyclist who thinks "hill work" means riding back and forth over the I-80 overpass. Cardiac is only a 1.7 mile climb at 6.3%, so don't worry about it. From the summit at mile **27.3** you may choose to return; otherwise continue another 6.5 enjoyable miles through oak forest to the end of this route at Moskowite Corner. The homey restaurant there serves ice cream too. Whichever return route you choose, watch for rocks in the road as you descend.

If you want more miles from Moskowite Corner, see ROUTES #13, #18, and #21.

2 WANDERIN' TO WINTERS _____

Starting Point: *Davis*
Distance: *21 miles one way*
Total Climb: *90 ft.*

Average Pavement Quality: *1.7*
Map: *Pages 12-13*

This isn't the quickest, but it is the quietest way from Davis to Winters. The quick and safe way is to take Road 31 all the way to Road 90A, then south as shown on the map. The purpose of this route, however, is to take you out into the vast open lands of Yolo County and to avoid using busy and narrow Russell Boulevard east of Winters. There is another benefit to riding in Yolo County: the good feeling from being out in the middle of working land, rich soil, and open sky. The roads of this route and adjacent roads can be used to create short training rides or to just get away from it all. Navigation is easy in Yolo County when you understand the mile square grid road system. For example, Road 99 to Road 95 equals four miles. Easy! This is not a hard-and-fast rule, however. Not all numbered roads connect or are exactly where they should be.

Start from Covell Boulevard at the Highway 113 overpass and go west. Covell changes names and becomes Road 31 there. After five miles turn north on Road 95 and continue past the Yolo County Airport. Turn west on Road 29, travel one mile, then north on Road 94, and after two miles turn west on Road 27. Rice and alfalfa are common crops out here, with some corn, tomatoes, and sugar beets also. Don't worry about the nice German shepherd on Road 27; he's on a chain, usually. Quickly turn south on Road 92D. A fast mile later, turn west on Road 28, your only option. Swing south again on Road 91B. At Road 29A head west just 0.4 mile, then south again on Road 90A down to Road 31. Yes, that's right, you did turn north away from Road 31 over twelve miles back.

Cross Road 31 and continue south alongside I-505 to Road 32 and turn west there. Go over the overpass and enter the little hamlet of Winters. I recommend the natural-foods sandwich shop on Railroad Avenue and the grocery on Main. A good return option would be using Putah Creek Road with 13.7 miles back to Davis (see ROUTE #1).

3 NORTH BY NORTHWEST _____

Starting Point: *Davis*
Distance: *27.6 miles one way*
Total Climb: *280 ft.*

Average Pavement Quality: *1.9*
Map: *Pages 12-13*

This is the quick and quiet way from Davis to Esparto. The highlight of the trip is a herd of camels on Road 23 near Esparto. Almost all of this route passes through unfenced farmlands with seasonal row crops such as wheat, corn, tomatoes, melons, and rice. This route can be used as an interesting training ride, as a connector to ROUTES #4 and #5, or as a nice family day ride in the country over to Esparto for lunch and back. A northwest wind makes this a bit of a challenge, but sailing effortlessly back to Davis is a real treat.

From Covell Boulevard at the Highway 113 overpass, turn north on the west side frontage road, Road 99D. Pass the golf course and turn west on Road 29. If you're hungry now, stop at Plainfield Station on Road 98 just north of Road 29 where they serve great burgers and beer. Continue west on curvy Road 29 to Road 95 just north of the Yolo County Airport. Travel two miles north to Road 27, then west again 7.1 miles all the way out to Road 88.

Yolo County—Road 93

As you probably noticed, all your turns are north, then west, and if you continue that pattern to Road 23 you won't get lost. On Road 26, look for the stately old house with a turret and palm trees.

When you turn west on Road 23, the camels will be on the right a mile and a half later. (If you want to rush into Esparto and skip all this fun, turn north on Road 86.) From the camels at mile **22.8** continue west up and over "Mt. Pushmore" (which towers a full 3,960 inches above the Yolo landscape). Then turn northeast on Road 22, which winds along a tree-lined creek and past small farms. Turn north at Road 85B, then immediatly east on Road 20A, which will take you directly into Esparto at the city park. I use this slightly roundabout approach because the pleasant scenery on Road 22 is worth the detour and the camels are a most unusual sight. Esparto has a grocery store on the south end, a burger stand across from the park, and my favorite, Marvin's Market and Deli in the north end of town. Many of the buildings in Esparto are old, some near one hundred years, like the one occupied by Marvin's Market. You may return the way you came or continue north on Road 87 (see ROUTE #5) or travel up Cache Creek to Guinda and beyond (see ROUTE #4).

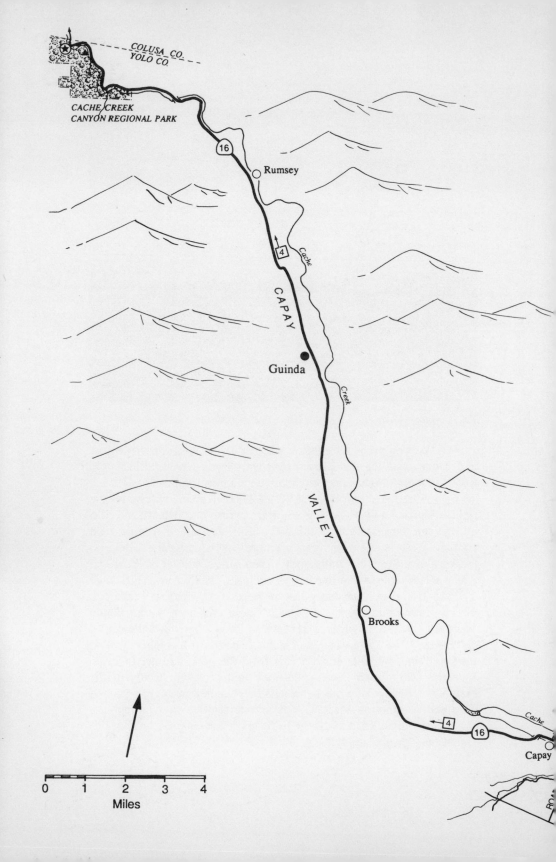

COLUSA CO.
YOLO CO.

CACHE CREEK
CANYON REGIONAL PARK

16

Rumsey

4

Cache

CAPAY

Guinda

Creek

VALLEY

Brooks

4

16

Cache

Capay

ROAD

0   1   2   3   4

Miles

4 CACHE CREEK EXPRESS _____

Starting Point: *Esparto*
Distance: *28.3 miles one way*
Total Climb: *560 ft.*

Average Pavement Quality: *1.7*
Map: *Pages 18-19*

This route goes from Esparto north through the Capay Valley, one of the oldest agricultural regions in the state because of its mild climate and easy access to water. Almonds and walnuts are major crops in the upper end of the valley with tomatoes, sorghum, and corn grown in the lower end. The route has its special seasons. Spring and fall are very colorful and warm in the river canyon, and the traffic is usually light. Watch in particular for the spectacular spring bloom of the almonds. On summer weekends Highway 16 can be quite busy with all the "tubers" heading for Cache Creek Park; the narrow shoulder is something to consider at these times. In the winter you can often enjoy the sunshine without the fog more prevalent in the Central Valley. Cache Creek is actually a good-sized river and quite popular with rafters, kayakers, and the "tubers" too. Cache Creek Canyon Regional Park near the Yolo County border is a good destination point with restrooms, water, and camping facilities. Guinda is the only town with a store from Esparto to Clear Lake, so plan accordingly.

From the city park in Esparto head west on Grafton Avenue which becomes Road 20A as you leave town. Turn north on Road 85B and follow it as it becomes Highway 16, then veers west through quiet Capay and into the Capay Valley. You will pass the new High-Stakes Bingo Parlour at Brooks run by a local Indian tribe. In Guinda, at mile **16.3**, there are two stores open seven days a week and a county park on the river. Rumsey, now just a wide spot in the road, is where the valley gives way to the dramatic river canyon. Ancient geologic strata are clearly visible here, having been exposed by the cutting action of the river through the centuries. The road climbs gradually as it navigates the canyon, finally reaching the first of the three-part Cache Creek Park at mile **26.3**. The second or "middle site" at mile **27.1** has pleasant camping facilities that would make an enjoyable overnight tour. The "upper site" is nothing more than a parking lot with river access. Cache Creek is the outflow for Clear Lake, so the water is usually quite warm in the summer. For more information on Cache Creek Park, contact the Yolo County Parks Department in Woodland.

I omitted the Colusa County portion of Highway 16 from the map due to space limitations. The profile does show the next 7.3 miles to the Highway 16 terminus at Highway 20. A wild tule elk range borders the road at that point, but I have seen only two of the reclusive beasts in all my travels there.

5A DUNNIGAN HILLS, SOUTHERN CROSSING _____

Starting Point: *Esparto*
Distance: *15.5 miles one way*
Total Climb: *80 ft.*

Average Pavement Quality: *1.8*
Map: *Pages 18-19*

This and the next two routes run between Esparto and Yolo. By using any two of them, you can create an interesting loop, thereby returning to Esparto. The Dunnigan Hills are a unique feature of Yolo County, resembling wrinkles in a carpet. The region is almost entirely wheat fields and grazing land with lots of rolling open hills in between. Morning can be a beautiful time to watch the light play across the undulating fields, especially in the hillier northern area. The vineyards in the central area add an interesting change of texture to the landscape.

The southern crossing begins, as do the next two, at the park in Esparto. Exit town to the north on Road 87, and after crossing the bridge over Cache Creek, turn east on Road 19. Seasonal row crops border the road until after the I-505 overcrossing where the terrain changes to grazing land for cattle and sheep. Look for the old schoolhouse on the left, 1.6 miles east of the overcrossing. Two small roller-coaster hills with rice fields between them mark the southern end of the Dunnigan Hills. Turn north on Road 95, then east on Road 18A, and enter an area of small family farms that fringe Woodland. Turn north again on Road 96B and follow it to the intersection with Road 17. Turn east there, continue over the I-5 overcrossing to the stop sign at Road 99W and Clarks Market, where food and a restroom can be found.

To continue south to Davis (another 16.2 miles), take Road 99W south to Road 18 and turn west. (See ROUTE #7 for directions from there.)

5B DUNNIGAN HILLS, OUT ZAMORA WAY _____

Starting Point: *Esparto*
Distance: *20.6 miles one way*
Total Climb: *110 ft.*

Average Pavement Quality: *2.0*
Map: *Pages 18-19*

As with the previous route, start at the park in Esparto and exit town via Road 87. Continue north past Road 19 to Road 16, where you turn east. Follow Road 16 through what feels like Oklahoma, cross I-505, veer north on Road 90B, then east on Road 15B. The crest lies just ahead as you turn north on Road 92B, passing a vineyard on your right. Don't worry about all those turns; there is no other paved way to go but this one. A short descent, on a road I'm sure Yolo County maintenance forgot about, will level out and eventually deposit you at Road 13, where you turn east. Zamora has a picturesque white church, a few well-kept homes, and not much else. Just south of the church, turn south on Road 94 just before the I-5 overcrossing. Pass huge plastic-covered piles of wheat before turning east on Road 14A. The fields to the east are often planted with watermelons, which ripen in the summer. Turn south again on Road 95 where ROUTE #5C joins at mile **15.7**. Turn east on Road 16, south on Road 96, and finally east on Road 17. This will take you into Yolo and Clarks Market on Road 99W.

5c DUNNIGAN HILLS, NORTHERN PASSAGE

Starting Point: *Esparto*
Distance: *35.2 miles one way*
Total Climb: *280 ft.*

Average Pavement Quality: *1.8*
Map: *Pages 18-19*

As with the previous two routes, begin at the park in Esparto. Travel north on Road 87 all the way up to Road 14 and turn west. After two miles turn north on Road 85, which takes you over two roller-coaster hills, through Bird Valley and past an old ranch, before turning east on Road 8. As the road veers north again, it becomes Road 86 where red-tailed hawks often soar on rising air currents. Gradually descend via what is now Road 6 into Dunnigan at mile **19.4**, passing service stations and a restaurant.

"Downtown" Dunnigan is just north on Road 99W and has a classic soda/sandwich counter in the general store. Road 99W is the frontage for I-5, which you may follow all the way to the town of Yolo if you like. But I recommend parting here and there to see some of the interesting agricultural land. Join with ROUTE #5B after crossing I-5 on Road 95 at mile **30.3** and continue jogging south and then east to Yolo and the store there. (See ROUTE #7 to continue south to Davis.)

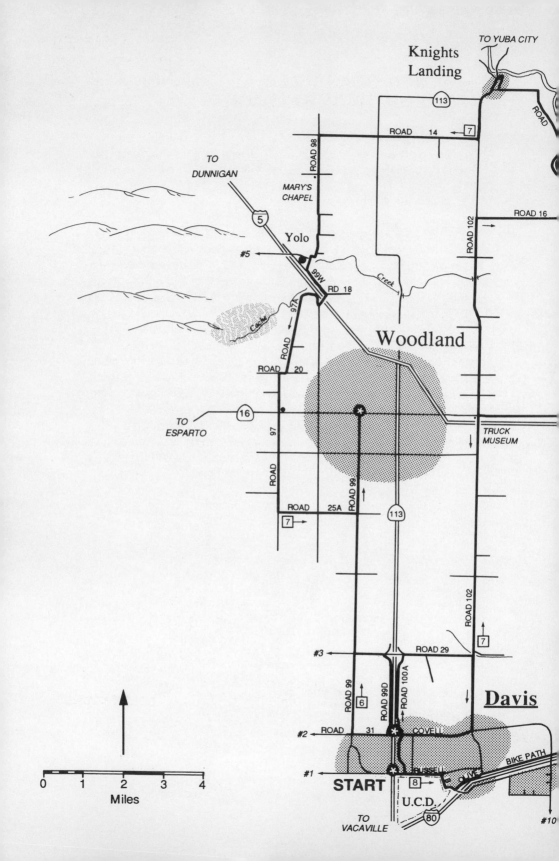

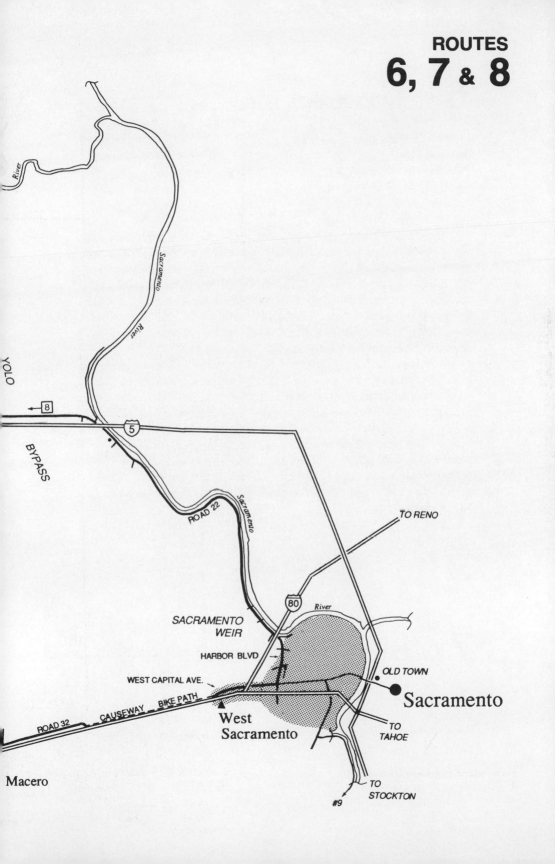

**ROUTES
6, 7 & 8**

River

Sacramento River

YOLO

8

5

BYPASS

ROAD 22

Sacramento

TO RENO

80

River

*SACRAMENTO
WEIR*

HARBOR BLVD

WEST CAPITAL AVE.

OLD TOWN

ROAD 32   CAUSEWAY   BIKE PATH

**West
Sacramento**

Sacramento

TO
TAHOE

Macero

#9

TO
STOCKTON

6 THE WAY TO WOODLAND _____

Starting Point: *Davis*
Distance: *9.1 miles one way*
Total Climb: *20 ft.*

Average Pavement Quality: *1.4*
Map: *Pages 24-25*

This, the shortest route in the book, shows a quick and safe way between Davis and Woodland. When people ask the best road, this is what I recommend. If you live on the east end of either Woodland or Davis, Road 102 is a good alternative (see ROUTE #7). I do *not* recommend riding on Road 98; it is much too busy with trucks and has no shoulder. For historians, Woodland is filled with beautiful turn-of-the-century homes. Fast-food delights abound in Woodland. A favorite Mexican restaurant is LaVilla on First Street, south of Main.

Begin heading west on Covell at Highway 113 for one mile to Road 99, turn north and pass the Sutter Davis Hospital. There is little or no shoulder from Road 31 four miles north to Road 27, so be alert for other traffic. The lines of olive trees north of Road 29 are probably all that remain from the grand entrance to a forgotten ranch estate. Maybe the home looked like the multistoried mansion at the intersection of Road 99 and Road 25A. Enter the Woodland city limits only **7.6** miles from Davis and cross Main Street another 1.5 miles north. The central part of town is to the east; a good bike shop can be found to the west.

7 KNIGHTS LANDING RAMBLE _____

Starting Point: *Davis*
Distance: *49.6 mile loop*
Total Climb: *130 ft.*

Average Pavement Quality: *1.7*
Map: *Pages 24-25*

The Knights Landing Ramble is an easy ride through the flat rural farmlands of eastern Yolo County. Historic Mary's Chapel north of Yolo has been in service for over 128 years and is one of the oldest churches in the state. The towns of Knights Landing and Yolo make good fuel stops and are historic sites in their own right. Occasional northerly winds can make this a bit of a challenge, sometimes even unpleasant, but remember, from Knights Landing it's tail-wind city all the way back.

Begin by heading east on Covell Boulevard at the Highway 113 overcrossing and immediately turn north on Sycamore Lane, also called Road 100A. At Road 29, turn east at the green Teichert tower and proceed to Road 102. Road 102 is an official Yolo County bike route, but the fast traffic does detract a bit from this portion. Travel north, skirting Woodland, and eventually cross over I-5, where two gas stations make handy water stops. After your break, continue north, then turn east on Road 16 at mile 15.2 and head over to the meandering Sacramento River. Turn north on tree-lined Road 116 atop the levee for good views of the river. As you enter Knights Landing, take a few minutes to view the old brick buildings by turning north on Railroad Street, then west on Second Street, south on Mill Street, and finally west on Fourth Street. There are many stores to choose from just south of here on Locust Street (also Highway 113). After refueling, exit town on Locust, head south and after crossing the bridge, turn west on Road 14. You may choose to return to Davis via Road 102, but you would only shave off four miles and miss sleepy little Yolo in the process. From Road 14 turn south on Road 98 and continue one mile to Mary's Chapel at mile 30.7. The shady lawn makes a cool nap spot on warm summer afternoons. Follow Road 98 south through a jog east at Road 16 and a jog west at Road 16A before turning west on Jackson Street and south on Main Street, into Yolo.

From the Elias Market on Main Street (open seven days), turn west on Clay Street, then south on Second Street and pass the school with a lawn and a table out front. After the railroad tracks, turn southeast on Road 99W. (At this point we are just south of Clarks Market where the Dunnigan Hills routes end.) Cross over I-5 on Road 18 and take the next right (north) just past the offramp to continue on Road 18. Olive trees line the road as you turn west up onto the levee beside Cache Creek. Exit the levee and turn south on Road 97A. Travel south two miles to Road 20, turn west, then make the next turn south on Road 97. Turn east at mile 40.9 on Road 25A at the elementary school, where water is available. Two miles later, turn south on Road 99 just past the big white house. This stretch of Road 99 is narrow, so be alert for other traffic. Turn east on Road 29, then south on Road 99D at the golf course. Finally, turn east on Road 31 and end at the overcrossing at Highway 113 and Covell. A shopping center, with plenty of refreshing possibilities, is half a mile east.

8 SACRAMENTO RIVER LOOP _____

Starting Point: *Davis*
Distance: *38.8 mile loop*
Total Climb: *90 ft.*

Average Pavement Quality: *1.4*
Map: *Pages 24-25*

This is a multipurpose route to use as the direct commute across the causeway or as a scenic ride along the river to Old Sacramento. The route as presented resembles a square. You can travel on the base of the square in an easterly direction across the causeway from Davis to Sacramento. This is not very aesthetic, I'm afraid, but it will get the job done. If you want a more scenic route to Sacramento and don't mind a **28.2**-mile trip, simply do ROUTE #8 clockwise.

Proceed east on Russell Boulevard from the Highway 113 overcrossing into town and turn south on B Street, then east on First Street. Continue through the tube under the railroad tracks to Olive Drive. Take Olive east to its termination at the freeway offramp, where the bike path begins. Travel east between the freeway and the tracks. Keep going east until mile **7.7**, at which time you follow the bike route signs over to the new causeway path and continue east to the other side. (The old Yolo Causeway bike path down below is often unusable in winter because of periodic flooding. The new bike path is elevated on the existing freeway.) The gas station in West Sacramento at mile **11.1** has water and restrooms. Continue on West Capital Avenue, riding east through an industrial neighborhood until Harbor Boulevard. If you're on your way to downtown Sacramento, or Old

Town, continue east another 2.1 miles to the fifty-year-old Tower Bridge and across the Sacramento River. Old Town Sacramento makes an enjoyable day ride destination with shops, restaurants, and the railroad museum.

If Sacramento isn't in your itinerary, turn north on Harbor Boulevard at mile **12.7**, cross some tracks, cross Reed Avenue, and cross another set of tracks. Just before passing under the I-80 bridge, continue north, now on Road 22. Road 22 travels the levee on the west side of the river. Cross the Sacramento Weir, a flood-control dam that diverts excess water into the Yolo Causeway area. Beyond the weir, Road 22 has little or no shoulder, so beware of other traffic. Cross under the Vietnam Veterans' Memorial Bridge at mile **22.1** and leave the river. Road 117 north of the bridge can be a very peaceful side trip along the river levee. This next portion of Road 22 can be closed during high water in winter, at which time the I-5 causeway may be used. Keep an eye out for wild pheasants in the rice fields along Road 22. The Hays Antique Truck Museum, another interesting diversion, is at the southward turn onto Road 102 where two gas stations have water and restrooms. Follow Road 102 for seven miles down to Covell Boulevard at the Carl's Jr. in Davis. Turn west there and continue 1.8 miles to Sycamore Lane. Take Sycamore south to Russell Boulevard then west again to the end point at Highway 113 and Russell.

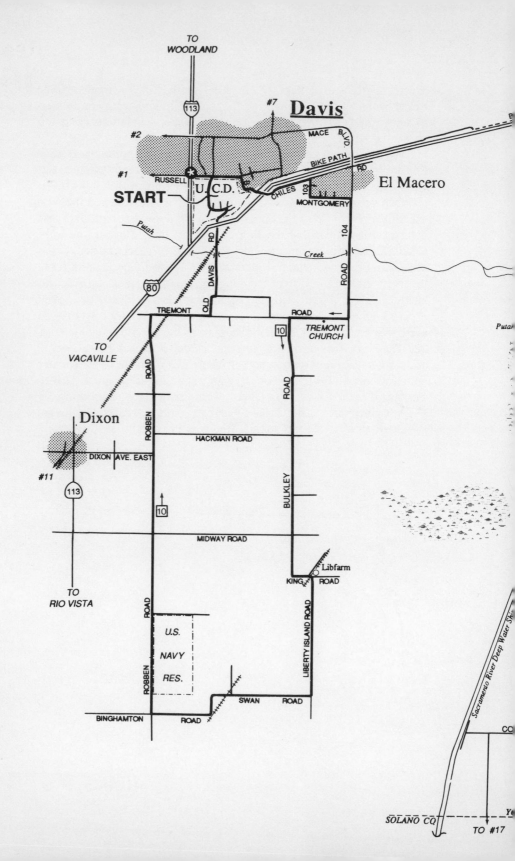

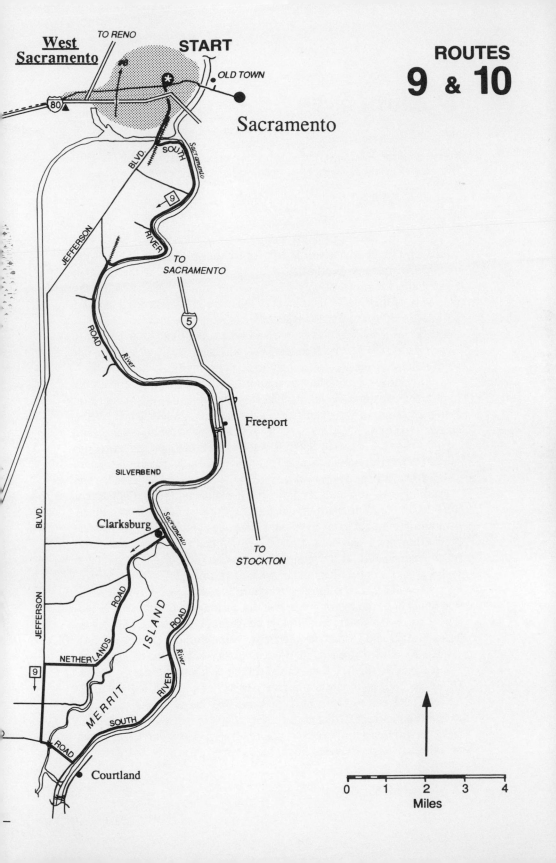

ROUTES
9 & 10

9 SOUTH RIVER

Starting Point: *West Sacramento*
Distance: *51 miles out & back*
Total Climb: *80 ft.*

Average Pavement Quality: *1.0*
Map: *Pages 30-31*

If the idea of pedaling along the Sacramento River appeals to you, then this is your ride. If fifty-one miles is too much, the total distance can easily be shortened by turning around at the store in Clarksburg, for a total of only 35.1 pleasant miles. The traffic on the west side of the river is light most of the time, but the road is narrow, so beware of other traffic, especially as you approach Clarksburg. South River Road can also be used to reach Rio Vista and the Sandy Beach Park campground (see ROUTES #17 and #16). Whatever your ability, South River Road is a quiet journey along the ol' Sacramento.

Finding a suitable starting point in West Sacramento is a bit of a task, but the Safeway parking lot on West Capital Avenue at Jefferson Boulevard will suffice. Take Jefferson south under all the freeway overpass mess, cross the drawbridge over the ship canal, and take the next left, east, on South River Road. From atop the levee, the views of the river and the fertile farmlands are wide and unobstructed. Drop down off the levee and turn south at the railroad trestle, then regain the levee at mile **8.2**. Silverbend makes an interesting stop at mile **16.0**. You'll find a fruit stand and a Christmas tree farm with its own miniature train to take you out to the trees and back. Pass a sugar-processing plant one mile south of Silverbend. In Clarksburg, 0.5 miles further south, is the quaint Holland Market (closed on Sundays) with a creaky wooden floor and country store smells.

After a nap on the shaded church lawn across from the store, you may choose to return north, thereby making your total 35.1 miles. Shady roads, however, and a slow peaceful river await to the south. Take Netherlands Road to Jefferson Boulevard (Highway 84). Continue south to Courtland Road and then take Courtland east to South River Road. The town of Courtland is across the river. Scenic Highway 160, also across the river, is too busy to be enjoyable by bicycle. Return to Clarksburg (another 7.5 miles north) via South River Road. From Clarksburg, simply continue on South River Road, and you will return to West Sacramento. To stay on South River Road, remember to turn east under the railroad trestle at Gregory Avenue.

10 FLYIN' DOWN TO SWAN ROAD

Starting Point: *Davis*
Distance: *40.5 mile loop*
Total Climb: *70 ft.*

Average Pavement Quality: *1.1*
Map: *Pages 30-31*

This route (actually in Solano County) is for the birds . . . hawks, starlings, quail, herons, ducks, ravens, swallows, and pheasants, to name but a few. On one trip along Bulkley Road, I lost count of all the egrets in just one field. You will also be pleasantly surprised by the high pavement quality, as well as the solitude, here in central Solano County. Total distances can easily be shortened by turning west on Tremont Road, Hackman Road, or Midway Road and heading back to Davis. The round-trip distances would then be about 16.5, 25.5, and 30.5 miles, respectively. There are no services along the route unless you travel to nearby Dixon. Spring and fall are the best seasons for bird watching and for mild temperatures, although summer evenings can be delightful too. For full-out, head-down training or an easy-paced ornithology jaunt, Flyin' Down to Swan Road is a good choice.

From Highway 113 at Russell Boulevard travel east past the U.C.Davis campus and turn south on B Street, then east on First Street. Go through the tube under the railroad tracks, across the freeway overpass, and continue east on Chiles Road to the blinking yellow light. Then turn south on Road 103. Follow Road 103 as it swings east and becomes Montgomery Avenue, south of the Willowbank tract. Then go south on Road 104 to Tremont Road and turn west. The Tremont Church at mile **8.6** is similar in age and architecture to Mary's Chapel mentioned in ROUTE #7, with a shady spot beside it too. Turn south on smooth and wide Bulkley Road and continue 6.5 miles to King Road, while looking for egrets in the rice fields to the east. Take King Road a half mile east past the large Valley Grain storage building, then turn south again on Liberty Island Road.

The Liberty Island Ferry was closed years ago after a levee road was damaged during high water. At the old ferry crossing, miles to the south, the ferrykeeper's house, rich with Delta memories, still stands overlooking the deserted loading ramp. Turn west on Swan Road at mile **19.7**, and take a moment to appreciate the openness, peace, and quiet. Swan Road swings south, becomes Bunker Station Road, then swings west and changes to Binghamton Road. This unique area is populated with gas wells, sugar beets, global communications radio towers, and a few thousand sheep. Take Robben Road north ten miles, straight as an arrow, back to Tremont Road. This can be a really fast ride if the wind has come up out of the south. Turn east at Tremont, then north again on Old Davis Road before crossing under I-80. Go straight on California Avenue at the Arboretum; then turn west on La Rue Road, which will lead you back to Russell Boulevard just east of Highway 113 where you began.

SOLANO COUNTY

SOLANO COUNTY
INTRODUCTION _____

Solano County offers a variety of cycling possibilities. Here you will find such contrasting features as vast agricultural lands similar to those in Yolo County; the Sacramento River Delta with its fertile islands, ferries, bridges, and the largest estuarine marshlands in the United States; quaint riverfront villages; hidden valleys with vineyards; miles of pear orchards; natural gas wells and oil refineries; and thriving communities with economic ties to neighboring military bases. It is this diversity and contrast that make Solano County an exciting place to explore on two wheels.

Fairfield is a population center, its expansion in recent years partly due to its connection with Travis Air Force Base to the east. The mammoth aircraft based there are often visible in the sky overhead. Vallejo, Solano County's largest urban area, is adjacent to another military base, Mare Island Naval Shipyard. Northeast of Fairfield is Vacaville (literally translated, "Cowtown"), also a growing community. Here you will find the famous I-80 freeway stop, The Nut Tree. Smaller riverfront towns such as Benicia, Suisun City, and Rio Vista are popular with sports fishermen and have other maritime industries. Dixon and Elmira, in central Solano County, are small, quiet agricultural towns.

The English Hills region just north of Vacaville is a favorite of cyclists in search of small but challenging hills, quiet roads, and rural beauty. The open expanses of northern Solano County are made more attractive by the miles of wide, smooth roads there. Solitude is the order of the day in southern Solano County too, where the Delta adds a unique marine flavor.

The same drawbacks present in Yolo County exist here too: agricultural burning, crop transportation, and crop dusting. (I should add that I have never had a problem with any of these hazards in either county, but the potential does exist.) Since cycling through large urban areas is not as enjoyable for me as country riding, I have steered clear of the few big cities as much as possible. Wind is prevalent in Solano County, especially near the water and through the narrow gaps in the hills when the Central Valley is heating up.

Solano County doesn't have awe-inspiring vistas, breath-taking beauty, or major tourist attractions. But its extensive open spaces, the subtlety and diversity of its landscape, and the lack of crowds can make this a valuable addition to your cycling itinerary.

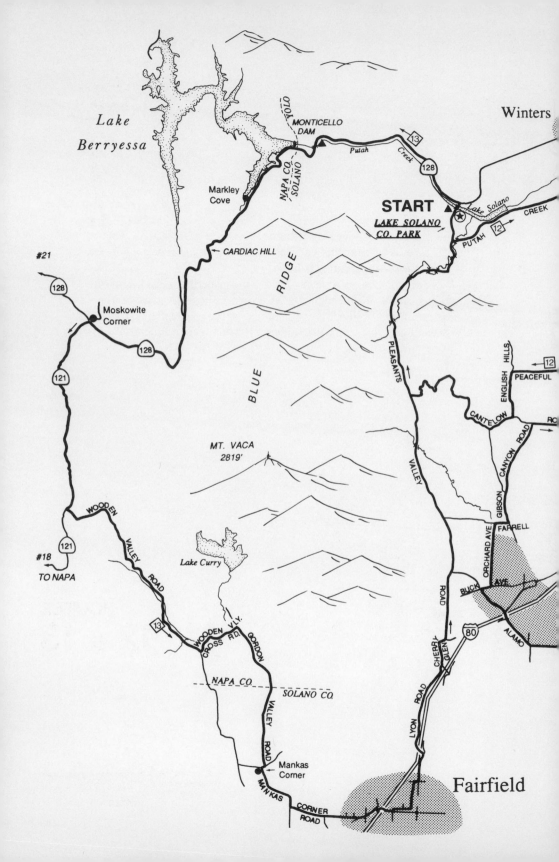

TO DUNNIGAN

TO WOODLAND

Davis

START **U.C.D.**

RUSSELL BLVD.

TO SAC.

#2

Creek

Putah

ROAD 32

YOLO CO.
SOLANO CO.

95A

ROAD

11

PUTAH   CREEK   ROAD

BOYCE   ROAD

BOW MAN

GADDINI

WINTERS RD.

113

WOLFSKILL

TUBBS   ROAD

SIEVERS   ROAD

STEVENSON BRIDGE ROAD

12

TREMONT

11

OLD   DAVIS   RD.

ROAD

11

NORTH   ROAD

SILVEYVILLE   ROAD

SCHROEDER

80

Dixon

ROBBEN   ROAD

ALLENDALE   ROAD

HARTLEY   ROAD

MERIDIAN   ROAD

DIXON   AVE   WEST

DIXON   AVE. EAST

#10

MIDWAY   ROAD

ROAD

113

PORTER   ROAD

80

505

ROAD

TO
RIO VISTA

S.P. R.R.

11

LEWIS   ROAD

TOWN   ROAD

acaville

LEISURE

ELMIRA RD.

HOLDENER
ROAD

Elmira

DRIVE

ROUTES
11, 12 & 13

0   1   2   3   4
Miles

11 THE COWTOWN CONNECTION

Starting Point: *Davis*
Distance: *57.3 mile loop*
Total Climb: *500 ft.*

Average Pavement Quality: *1.4*
Map: *Pages 38-39*

This route will take you out among fertile fields, through two small towns and one large one, and into some gentle hills dotted with apricot trees. The return to Davis is through dense walnut and almond groves. Spring time is spectacular, but any season can be a good time to ride in northern Solano County. Food and water can be found at regular intervals along the route, but be sure to stop at Fry's Grocery (open seven days) in Elmira for a cold drink and a rest in the shade. The stretch through Vacaville, although quick, can be busy, so take it easy there. (You can bypass Vacaville by turning north on Leisure Town Road to Tubbs Road. Another worthy addition, if you are so "inclined," is the 8.3% climb up western Cantelow Road; see ROUTE #12.)

From Highway 113 at Russell Boulevard go east to LaRue Road, then south to California Avenue, and straight on Old Davis Road out into the country. Take Tremont Road west to Robben Road, then head south to Dixon Avenue East, which will lead you west through the bustling town of Dixon. Pass a small market just before crossing First Street (Highway 113). Other food options are available to the north. George's Orange Mexican Restaurant, a personal favorite, can be found west of town on Dixon Avenue West near I-80. After crossing First Street, then the railroad tracks, turn southwest onto Porter Road and follow it to Midway Road at mile **14.4**. Travel west on Midway, then veer south before the freeway onto Lewis Road. Follow Lewis to Holdener Road, turn west, and proceed into Elmira at mile **22.0**.

Sleepy little towns like Elmira are a reminder of the small farm way of life slowly vanishing from the Central Valley. Reputedly, Elmira was nothing but raucus drinking establishments for nearby Vacaville when it was a dry town. Leave Elmira by turning west on Elmira Road. Watch for broken pavement. Turn south on Leisure Town Road at the rapidly expanding periphery of Vacaville, swing west on Alamo Drive, and pass a new shopping center with a Raley's and an ice cream parlor. Follow Alamo Drive west across the freeway, past another shopping center, before turning east on Buck Avenue at the stop sign. Turn north immediately on Orchard Avenue, then east again on Farrell Road over the old concrete bridge. At mile **31.6** turn north on Gibson Canyon Road and enter a semirural area also being rapidly developed.

The climb over the little summit is easy and the descent is fast before the turn east on Cantelow Road. To the west is the 810-foot summit if you desire more climbing. Veer north briefly on Timm Road, then go immediately east on Midway Road, which is narrow and can have fast traffic at times. The Oats Store at mile **36.7** is open seven days a week but has no fresh produce. Turn north just past the store onto Hartley Road, which parallels I-505. Continue to Allendale Road where you turn east under the freeway. Take the next road north, Tubbs Road, which also parallels the freeway. Turn east on Wolfskill Road, named for an early landowner, and enter an area of well-established apricot and walnut orchards. Travel north on Gaddini Road, then turn east on Bowman Road and go past a beautiful old house nestled in an orchard. Turn north again on Boyce Road, which runs through a dense walnut grove, before turning east at mile **45.4** on Putah Creek Road. Follow Putah Creek Road nearly six miles to Stevenson Bridge Road, turn north and cross the bridge into Yolo County. Turn east for the last time on Road 32 (also Russell Boulevard) where you can take the bike path all the way back to Davis at Highway 113 and Russell Boulevard in Davis.

12 GOOD OL' CANTELOW LOOP

Starting Point: *Davis*
Distance: *49.7 mile loop*
Total Climb: *930 ft.*

Average Pavement Quality: *1.7*
Map: *Pages 38-39*

The English Hills area is another favorite of Davis cyclists. It's fairly close, the hills are a bit of a challenge, the traffic is light, and the scenery is beautiful. The summit of Cantelow Road at 810 feet is the loftiest piece of asphalt in Solano County. The visibility east on those post-rain days can be a hundred miles or more. Cantelow Road is also the steepest road in Solano County, the east side averaging 6.1% with a short 10.6% pitch before the summit; the west side is a more sustained climb, averaging 8.3% from top to bottom. Pleasants Valley to the west of the English Hills is a small, quiet agricultural area with walnut and cherry orchards. Wind can often determine the direction you travel this loop. I like to start into the wind whenever possible.

Begin at Russell Boulevard and Highway 113 and follow the bike path west to Road 95A, just as in ROUTE #1. After crossing Stevenson Bridge, continue south *past* Putah Creek Road down to Sievers Road. Turn west there, then immediately south on Schroeder Road down to Silveyville Road, then west. After three miles, turn south on Meridian Road North, then west on Allendale Road, which crosses under I-505 at mile **16.2**. The English Hills are just beginning as you turn south on Timm Road. Turn west onto smooth and curvy Peaceful Glen Road. After two small rollers to warm your calves, veer south on English Hills Road. Continue over more easy rollers to the stop sign, then turn west onto Cantelow Road. The climb up Cantelow Road has enough elevation gain to be a challenge, yet overall is gentle enough for almost any cyclist. The "real steep" part is a short 10.6% pitch just before the summit, but it's only a quarter mile long! There are houses in this area with water, if you ask.

Take a little breather on top before the rapid drop down the west side. You're halfway at mile **25.4**. Be sure your brakes are in good shape because if the steepness doesn't get you, the old gravel patch halfway down will. Turn north on Pleasants Valley Road and begin to descend gently down the valley through an arbor of stately walnuts. Cross three narrow bridges before turning east on Putah Creek Road. Stay with Putah Creek Road all the way to Winters Road, which jogs north at mile **36.3**. After a quarter mile continue east on Putah Creek Road and go all the way back to Stevenson Bridge Road. Now turn north, cross the bridge, and enter Yolo County. Head east on Road 32, or the bike path if you choose, back into Davis.

Pleasants Valley Road (near Cantelow Road)

13 ONCE AROUND THE MOUNTAIN _____

Starting Point: *Lake Solano Co. Park*
Distance: *54.7 mile loop*
Total Climb: *2,250 ft.*

Average Pavement Quality: *1.2*
Map: *Pages 38-39*

     I was first introduced to this route by the Davis Bike Clubs' Fall Century in 1980. The Wooden Valley area west of Mt. Vaca has become a lasting favorite. Miles of vineyards turning bright colors every fall are a visual delight. Mankas Corner Deli and Restaurant, just over halfway around, makes a perfect lunch stop. It is open daily, 9 am to 6 pm. The route through Fairfield and Vacaville is the quickest and least congested way possible. Cyclists from these and surrounding communities can simply hook in wherever convenient. One drawback to this route is that Pleasants Valley Road is narrow and can have fast traffic and less than ideal sight distance, so be extra careful there. Beginning cyclists might want to avoid southern Pleasants Valley until riding skills around cars become sharp.

     Start this route at Lake Solano County Park, which has restrooms and water. Parking costs two dollars. Exit north and turn west on Highway 128 toward Lake Berryessa. Climb up to the dam and stop to take a look down into the "glory hole," or overflow pipe; wouldn't that make a great amusement park ride, once! Begin to ascend good ol' Cardiac Hill at the Markley Cove Store and reach the summit 1.7 miles later at 1,030 feet. Rocks often fall onto the road from the exposed hillsides, so watch out for them as you descend. At Moskowite Corner there is a restaurant, store, and gas station. Swing south here onto Highway 121 at mile **16.0** toward Napa. After passing Circle Oaks Drive, climb a little hill, then drop quickly into Wooden Valley. Some of the corners in the descent are not well engineered, so watch your speed the first time through. The road flattens before a little drop to the junction of Wooden Valley Road. This corner can be tricky too, as you turn south across "blind" traffic. Sail down Wooden Valley Road between vineyards and then alongside a small brook, before turning east on Wooden Valley Cross Road at mile **27.3**. This turn is easy to miss, so be sure to watch for it. Turn south onto Gordon Valley Road and climb a bit, then descend through more vineyards and orchards before arriving at Mankas Corner Deli in fine fashion. Also, small roadside fruit stands appear in summer and fall, so be sure to take advantage of them.

After lunch, travel south on Mankas Corner Road. Turn east at mile **34.0** to stay on Mankas Corner Road, and continue to Fairfield. Bear left as the road becomes Waterman Boulevard (no sign), now surrounded by new homes with more under construction. Turn south to cross the I-80 freeway at Hilborn. This is a tricky spot to navigate because you must travel where cars exit and enter the freeway at high speeds. Go east over the overpass and begin Air Base Parkway, then take the very next turn north on Heath Drive at the signal. Turn immediately east on Dahlia Street, which later veers north and becomes Orchid Street. Follow Orchid to its end at Marigold Drive, then go east to North Texas Street. Take North Texas north, past a drive-in, back across I-80, then north on Lyon Road. Lyon is a frontage road that ends at Cherry Glen Road near the Vacaville glider airport. Take Cherry Glen Road north 0.8 mile. Then turn north (left) on Pleasants Valley Road. Be cautious on this stretch because the road has no shoulder. Stay with Pleasants Valley Road for the next 12.5 miles back to Lake Solano Park where you began. Luckily the road becomes less traveled the farther north you go.

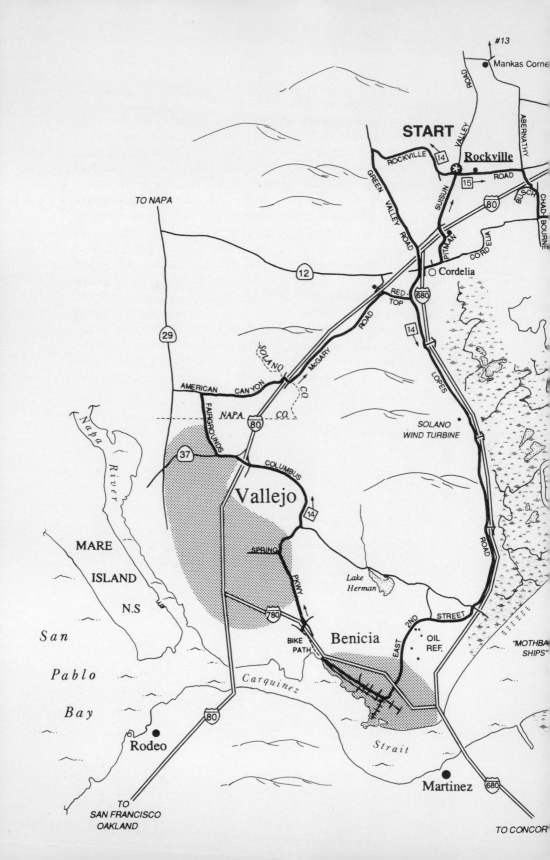

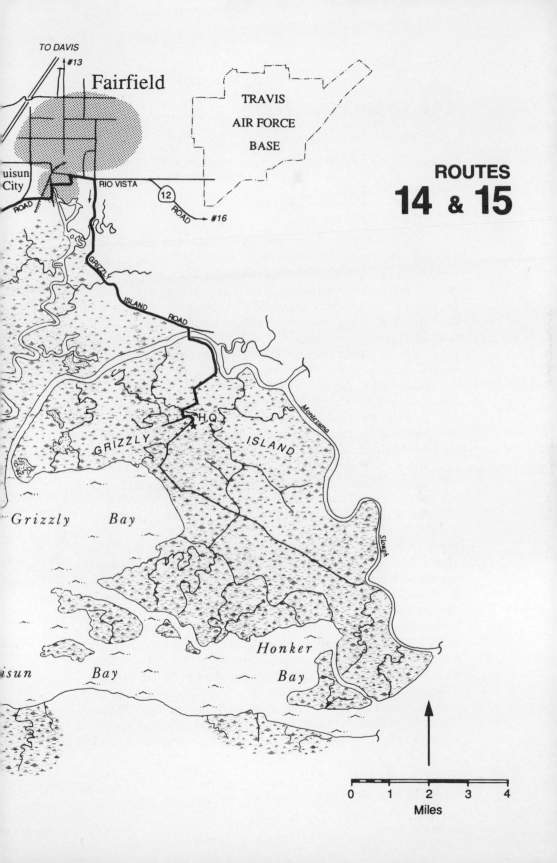

TO DAVIS

#13

Fairfield

TRAVIS
AIR FORCE
BASE

ROUTES
14 & **15**

uisun
City

RIO VISTA

12

ROAD

#16

ROAD

GRIZZLY

ISLAND ROAD

Montezuma

HQ

ISLAND

GRIZZLY

Grizzly Bay

Slough

Honker

isun Bay

Bay

0   1   2   3   4
Miles

14 WHIRLWIND TOUR _____

Starting Point: *Rockville*   **Average Pavement Quality:** *1.6*
Distance: *40.9 mile loop*   **Map:** *Pages 46-47*
Total Climb: *1,340 ft.*

This enjoyable figure-eight ride will take you past a high-tech 300-foot wind turbine, the mothball fleet, an oil refinery, and the historic waterfront town of Benicia--all in the first twenty miles. The massive wind turbine was built here for a good reason: wind. Many of the trees along the freeway and on the mountain have been sculpted by this tireless force and now look like huge Japanese bonsai. West to east is the prevailing wind direction, due to the temperature differential between the hot Central Valley and cool San Francisco Bay. It is not always windy here, however. Spring and fall are great times, with many calm days. Be sure to explore First Street in Benicia with restaurants, cafes, antique shops, galleries, and much more.

From the small town of Rockville, take Rockville Road west over the hill where the scars of a stone quarry can be seen. Turn south on Green Valley Road, which narrows to no shoulder. Continue to the I-80 freeway overcrossing where the road name changes to Lopes Road. Follow Lopes Road along the west side of Freeway 680. At mile **10.2** the Solano Wind Turbine is an impressive sight. When the wind generator is operating, the tips of the blades travel about two hundred miles an hour.

Cross Lake Herman Road and begin East Second Street at mile **15.4** with an overlook of the mothball ships at anchor in Suisun Bay (pronounced Soo-soon) to the south. Ascend a small hill overlooking the Exxon oil facility, then descend quickly, cross under Freeway 780, and enter Benicia. Turn west on Military East, then south on First Street, a short distance later. If you want to eat, explore, or rest in a shady park, continue downtown from here and rejoin the route later. If not, turn west on K Street and continue to the enterance of Benicia State Recreation Area, and drop down into the parking lot. Follow the bike path, which exits from the far end of the lot. At the end of the path, turn north on State Park Road, cross back over the 780 Freeway and continue north on Columbus Parkway toward Vallejo. Veer north again away from Springs Road (watch for this) and climb a short hill.

Stay with Columbus Parkway over two more little climbs, past a golf course, and then descend to what looks like a forced entry onto I-80. Have no fear, you're going across I-80. Just keep taking the left options, not the I-80 east or west onramps, and follow the sign for Highway 37.

Once safely across, merge right, watch for exiting traffic, and continue a bit more to Fairgrounds Drive and turn north at the signal. Stay on Fairgrounds and cross the Napa County line where the road narrows to one lane. Turn east on American Canyon Road at mile **30.2.** American Canyon climbs nicely, reenters Solano County, and recrosses I-80. Turn east on McGary Road, which descends for four miles along the south side of the freeway. The wind is often out of the west, which proves cycling is not always uphill and against the wind! At Red Top Road turn east away from the freeway, descend a bit more to Lopes Road, and turn north there. After crossing the tracks, turn east into Cordelia and follow Cordelia Road to Pittman Road. Pittman crosses I-80, where all the gas stations and fast food places cluster, then changes to Suisun Valley Road on the north side of the freeway. Suisun Valley Road will lead you past the new Solano County Community College and back to Rockville where a store awaits you.

15 GRIZZLY ISLAND VISTAS _____

Starting Point: *Rockville*
Distance: *33 mile loop*
Total Climb: *140 ft.*

Average Pavement Quality: *1.7*
Map: *Pages 46-47*

Here is a route to ride slowly while enjoying the views. Grizzly Island has levees, sloughs and salt marshes, cattle, and ducks. This ride is not for skinny tires, however. The pavement is generally not that good, and there is some hardpack gravel; anything from touring tires to balloon tires would be suitable. The first portion of the route from Rockville to Fairfield can be used as a connector to ROUTE #16 and points east. As in all of Solano County, wind can be a factor, especially during the hot summer months. Also, because most of the area is peat soil, the road bounces and vibrates when a heavy vehicle passes over it. (However, I don't recommend lying in the road to get a massage if a truck passes.)

From Rockville, take wide-shouldered Rockville Road east out past Iwama Market. Take Abernathy Road south, cross I-80, and turn south to continue on Abernathy away from the I-80 onramp. Turn east on Busch Drive, then immediately south onto the divided four-lane Chadbourne Road. Turn east again on Cordelia Road and pass a turf farm to the south. Enter Suisun City as you cross a set of railroad tracks at mile **5.2**. Turn north onto Main Street where you'll find a grocery on the left. After a short distance take Louisiana Street east, then a few blocks later turn north on Marina Boulevard. Travel east on Rio Vista Road (Highway 12) for 0.6 mile before turning south on Grizzly Island Road at the shopping center. The road is narrow and bumpy in places, but the open expanses and salt air more than

Montezuma Hills Road (near Birds Landing)

compensate. Fishing is a popular activity, or should I say lack of activity, on Grizzly Island. The headquarters for the Grizzly Island Wildlife Area is 9.2 miles from Highway 12, with water, an outhouse, and a phone next to the information office. There are another nine miles of good gravel road if you wish to continue. To return, do what you just did, only do it in the other direction.

For a shorter trip into Grizzly Island Wildlife Area, start at the Sunset Shopping Center in Fairfield. This would make the total distance only **18.4** miles out and back.

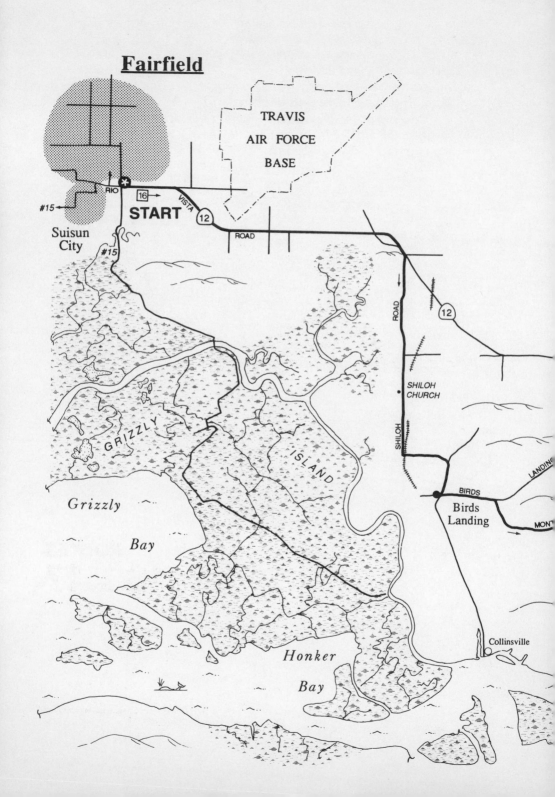

Fairfield

TRAVIS
AIR FORCE
BASE

RIO

16 →

START

12

VISTA

ROAD

#15 →

Suisun
City

#15

12

ROAD

SHILOH

SHILOH
CHURCH

LANDING

BIRDS

Birds
Landing

MONT

GRIZZLY

ISLAND

Grizzly

Bay

Collinsville

Honker

Bay

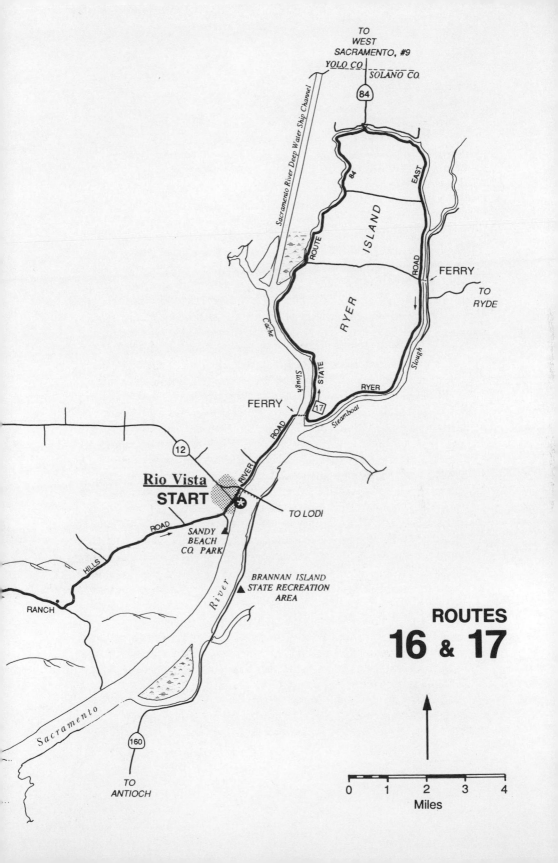

TO
WEST
SACRAMENTO, #9
YOLO CO.
SOLANO CO.

84

Sacramento River Deep Water Ship Channel

84

EAST

ISLAND

RYER

ROUTE

STATE

FERRY

TO
RYDE

Cache

Slough

Slough

RYER

FERRY

ROAD

17

Steamboat

12

RIVER

Rio Vista
START

ROAD

TO LODI

ROAD

SANDY
BEACH
CO. PARK

HILLS

RANCH

River

BRANNAN ISLAND
STATE RECREATION
AREA

Sacramento

160

TO
ANTIOCH

ROUTES
16 & 17

0   1   2   3   4
Miles

16 THE ROAD
   TO RIO .... VISTA _____

Starting Point: *Fairfield*
Distance: *27 miles one way*
Total Climb: *560 ft.*

Average Pavement Quality: *1.5*
Map: *Pages 52-53*

The gentle Montezuma Hills are a beautiful feature of southern Solano County. Primarily a wheat-growing and sheep-grazing region, it has a feeling similar to that found in the Dunnigan Hills (see ROUTES #5A, #5B, and #5C). There is a definite maritime flavor present--salt air, rushes, boats passing by--especially in Collinsville and Rio Vista. This route can be used for an out-and-back day ride, a connection from Fairfield to points east, or a weekend camp-out at Sandy Beach County Park. Since Highway 12 east of Shiloh Road is much too narrow to be safe, let alone enjoyable, this is the only usable biking route between Fairfield and Rio Vista. The rolling hills shelter some of the route from the summer westerly winds.

Begin at the Sunset Shopping Center in Fairfield where you will find a Lucky Store, a McDonald's, an ice cream shop, etc. Proceed east on Highway 12, with its wide shoulder, toward Travis Air Force Base. Veer south onto Shiloh Road at mile **7.8** and head out into the rolling open lands of southern Solano County. The Shiloh Church, 3.6 miles south, is over 110 years old. Swing east and cross abandoned railroad tracks at mile **13.0**. The hills rise and fall below you. Descending into Birds Landing at mile **15.0**. Be sure to stop at Benjamin's Store (open seven days) for a cool drink and some local humor. Built in 1875, it is, according to the proprietor, "the Safeway of Birds Landing!" This is a must stop. If you have the time, head down to Collinsville (eight miles out and back) to see the river and the houses built on stilts. To continue to Rio Vista, take Birds Landing Road east 1.4 miles to Montezuma Hills Road and turn south. The last time I looked, there were two short gravel patches just ahead, but they weren't a problem. The ranches in this area look well cared for with their fresh coats of paint and protective stands of eucalyptus trees. After a few pleasant climbs and drops, leave the hills and enter Rio Vista at mile **26.4**. Sandy Beach County Park is 0.7 mile to the south, with water and restrooms ($2.00 day use, $6.00 per site overnight). Veer north onto South Second Street, past well-kept houses, before turning east on Main Street to the end point at City Hall and the water's edge. The Point Restaurant is highly recommended by the locals. To ride along the river or to continue north to Sacramento, see ROUTES #17 and #9.

17 RIVER LEVEE, RYER FERRY

Starting Point: *Rio Vista*
Distance: *25.6 mile loop*
Total Climb: *20 ft.*

Average Pavement Quality: *2.0*
Map: *Pages 52-53*

This route is similar to ROUTE #9, but there are some notable differences. Ryer Island is more natural, or maybe less disturbed says it better. This is without question the flattest of all the routes presented. The only "hills" are the access ramps to and from the Ryer Island Ferry. The ferries are small, riding low in the water, carrying four to six cars or trucks at a time. Ferry operators do take a long lunch break, however, sometimes as long as an hour. There is no charge for the two-minute journey across Cache Slough, which was the second home to Humphrey the humpback whale. Rio Vista has plenty of parking on the street and in the public boat ramp parking lot just behind City Hall. Restrooms, water, and a phone are there too. (City Hall is easy to find. Take the Main Street exit from eastbound Highway 12 and go right down to the river.) The Food Fair grocery (open 7 am to 9 pm, seven days) is three short blocks west, also on Main Street.

From Rio Vista City Hall ride west just a few hundred feet to Front Street and turn north. Pass the Rio Vista Museum, a farm hardware store, and a pizza place before crossing under Highway 12 and turning east on River Road. Be cautious on this narrow stretch as it winds along only a few feet above the river. Board the ferry at mile **2.6** and obey any instructions of the ferry operator when disembarking on the other side. The direction of travel around Ryer Island is really up to you, but if you want to be on the inland side of the levee, ride clockwise. The road to the north (State Route 84) takes you alongside Cache Slough, where full-sized ships on their way to Port Sacramento are a common sight.

At mile **9.7** a large steel building clings to the inland side of the levee. The marshes in this area are largely undisturbed and are home to many bird species. Continue 2.5 miles farther, leave S.R. 84 and proceed straight on Ryer Road East, which is just south of a white drawbridge. If you're on your way to Courtland or points north, cross the bridge and exit the levee onto Courtland Road (see ROUTE #9). There's not a lot going on around here other than farmin' and fishin'. For an interesting side trip, take the Howard Landing Ferry, at mile **17.3**, for a seven-mile loop to Ryde to see the famous Ryde Hotel. Otherwise, complete your Ryer Island tour at mile **23.0**, which brings you back to the Ryer Island Ferry only 2.6 miles from Rio Vista. The city park south of Main between 3rd and 4th has shady lawns and a swimming pool.

NAPA
COUNTY

NAPA COUNTY
INTRODUCTION _____

The amazing thing about Napa County is that, despite the appeal of its wineries and vineyards, you can still find cycling roads all to yourself. I'm sure many people in the area feel that Napa Valley's world-famous beauty and mystique amount to mostly a pain in the rear, especially when they're sitting in the middle of a Saturday afternoon traffic jam in St. Helena. Obviously, I feel the summer tourist season is not the best time to ply some of these routes.

The "wine country mystique" does, however, provide one nice benefit to cyclists: substantial tax revenues, which the county spends on maintaining some of the finest roads anywhere. Indeed, the truly great cycling roads of this county (and there are many) are not within the Napa Valley itself but in the hills and valleys that surround it. In that light, I have done my best to skirt or shoot through the few urban centers in the Napa Valley. Napa is the largest city in the county and spreads clear across the wide southern end of the valley. Calistoga, in the northern end, is much smaller and is famous for mud baths and glider rides. St. Helena, just south of Calistoga and also on the west side of the valley, is not as touristy as Calistoga and still retains a certain charm. Smaller towns such as Yountville, Oakville, and Rutherford are famous for their wineries and historical stone buildings. The Silverado Trail runs the length of the valley on the eastern flank and provides pleasant vistas over the acres of vineyards. The main drawback to this wide and smooth road, however, is the fast and often heavy summer traffic. Napa County does have the honor of possessing both the steepest climb (16%+ on Oakville Grade) and the most sustained drop (1,800 feet in 5.9 miles on Highway 29) to be found in this guide. Unfortunately, they're not on the same route.

The wind is rarely a problem outside of the Napa Valley, but within the valley it can be fairly strong, especially in the afternoons. Temperatures reflect the southerly wind pattern here, with summer highs at least ten degrees warmer in the northern end of the valley.

Also, it can be quite nippy on spring and fall mornings in the protected valleys and higher roads near Lake Berryessa. Winter snow is rare but not unheard of in Angwin, on Mt. Veeder Road, on Atlas Peak Road, and on Mt. St. Helena.

Lake Berryessa is a very beautiful lake, but its popularity is a negative factor as far as cycling is concerned. The only advice I can give here is to avoid the main access roads and all the "gotta get to the lake" traffic on peak summer weekends.

The roads surrounding the little town of Pope Valley are as close to perfect for cycling as any in the state: smooth, wide, challenging, lightly traveled, and truly beautiful. When I think of the best that cycling has to offer, I think of Napa County and of these miles of quiet roads among the oaks.

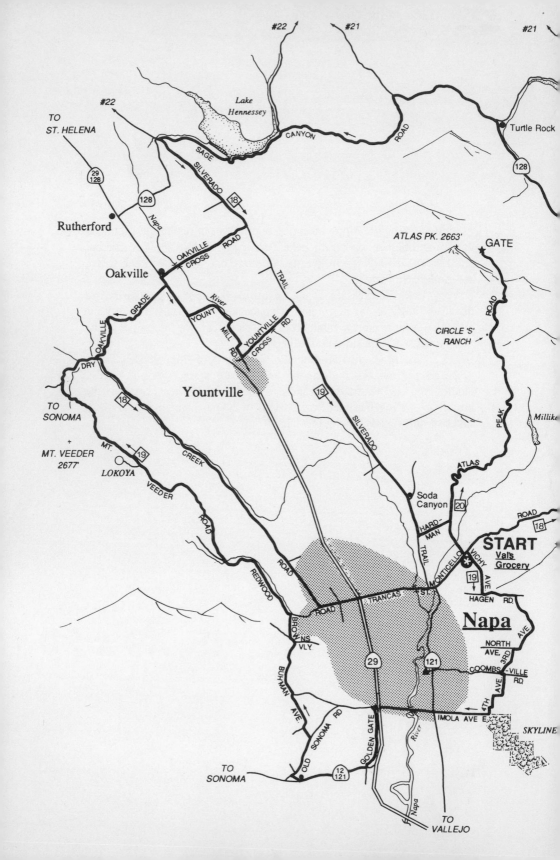

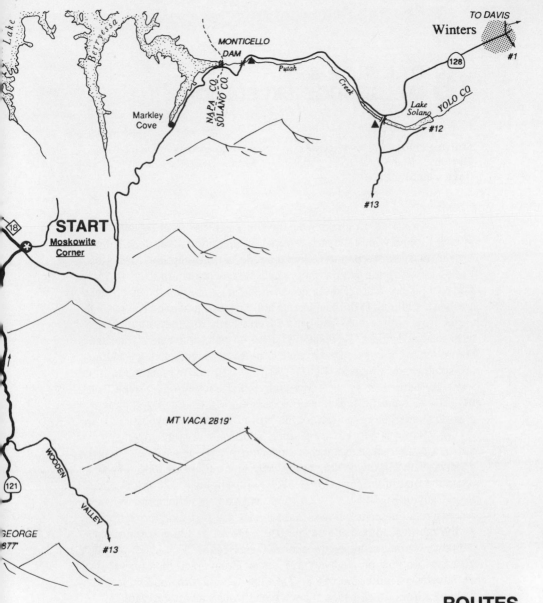

Lake

Berryessa

Lake

TO DAVIS

Winters

#1

MONTICELLO
DAM

Putah

128

Creek

Lake
Solano

YOLO CO.

#12

Markley
Cove

NAPA CO.
SOLANO CO.

#13

18

START

Moskowite
Corner

MT VACA 2819'

WOODEN

121

VALLEY

GEORGE
677'

#13

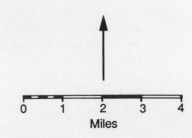

ROUTES
18, 19 & 20

0   1   2   3   4

Miles

18 OAKVILLE & MT. GEORGE EXPEDITION _____

Starting Point: *Moskowite Corner*
Distance: *49.6 mile loop*
Total Climb: *2,900 ft.*

Average Pavement Quality: *1.3*
Map: *Pages 60-61*

This ride will take you up and over the steepest piece of asphalt I found within the area covered by this book. Any road called "grade" must be steep, and Oakville Grade is no exception, averaging 13.5% for one mile with a short pitch before the summit of 16.2%. The route is not that difficult, however, because the four steep climbs are short, while most of the descents are long and gradual. The terrain varies from rolling oak- and pine-covered hills to vineyards to cool, redwood-lined creeks. There are two stores enroute, conveniently located before the big climbs. This route can be easily lengthened by adding the southwestern parts of ROUTE #19. If you really want some hill work, try adding on Howell Mountain Road above Pope Valley (see ROUTES #22 and #23). But the Oakville and Mt. George Expedition is a worthy undertaking in itself for the "upwardly mobile" cyclist.

Begin at Moskowite Corner, which has a store (open seven days), a restaurant, and a gas station with plenty of parking. Travel northwest on Highway 128, pass Turtle Rock Store at mile **4.8**, and begin the first of the four climbs. Stay with Highway 128 (also called Sage Canyon Road) another 3.4 miles and pass the Nichellini Winery where a rapid descent follows. Take it easy the first time through; one of the corners comes at you quickly. Down at Lake Hennessey, continue southwest along the shore where solitary fishermen ply the waters. Continue on Highway 128 below Conn Dam, then turn south on Silverado Trail at mile **16.0**. Take the second turn southwest onto Oakville Cross Road, which slices a path through a vast vineyard.

When you reach Highway 29, just north of you is the Oakville Grocery (10 am to 6 pm, seven days), which has a classic wooden floor and a good produce selection for a refreshing snack. Take Highway 29 south just 0.2 mile, then head west through more grapes below the looming Oakville Grade. I really can't think of any advice to make this little hill easier. But don't zigzag, it looks bad; falling over is better. At the summit, swear you'll never do that again, then descend to the bottom, where you turn abruptly south onto Dry Creek Road at mile

25.2. Dry Creek rolls and plays for nine miles in the shade of oaks, madrones, and scattered redwoods before depositing you among houses where you turn east on Redwood Road.

Take Redwood across Highway 29 where it becomes Trancas Street and continue straight through town. There is a good bike shop just west of Highway 29 in the Redwood Plaza on the right. Stay with Trancas past the hospital, past Silverado Trail to the stop sign at Highway 121. Trancas Road becomes Monticello Road at mile **37.1**. Monticello is flat at first and passes two roadside markets. The second one, at Vichy Avenue, is the starting point for ROUTES #19 and #20. Be sure to have plenty of water on board for the long climb up Mt. George. It's never very steep, but the narrow road and fast traffic can be a pain. Reach the summit 3.2 miles later, followed by an exhilarating plunge into Wooden Valley. Another short, narrow climb and a quick descent will take you into Capell Valley and back to Moskowite Corner for a well-deserved scoop of ice cream. Make it a double!

19 MT. VEEDER QUEST _____

Starting Point: *Napa*
Distance: *46 mile loop*
Total Climb: *2,060 ft.*

Average Pavement Quality: *1.3*
Map: *Pages 60-61*

If you want to tour a less beaten path in the Napa area or do a challenging half-day ride through quiet hills and vineyards, this is the route. You will circle north and east of Napa, passing lovely homes and miniranches before crossing the Napa River. The rolling vineyards east of Sonoma quickly give way to cool, shaded Redwood Canyon, where you climb Mt. Veeder Road to Lokoya. The views, the quiet, and the forest smells make for a wonderful journey. Flying down the steep 13.5% east face of Oakville Grade is a thrilling way to reenter the Napa Valley. Yountville has many small shops to browse in and cafes for refreshments before striking out into the grapes. Silverado Trail is wide and smooth, but the tourist traffic can be heavy on warm weekends. Pass the famous Silverado Country Club before returning to the roadside grocery where you began.

Start at Val's Grocery where Vichy Avenue intersects Monticello Road (Highway 121). Val's is open from 7 am to 9 pm, seven days a week, with plenty of parking and a water faucet out back. The next six miles have some confusing turns and road name changes, so follow these directions carefully. Take Vichy Avenue south to the stop sign and turn east onto Hagen Road. Veer south on 3rd Avenue, which passes through a vineyard at mile **3.0**. Stay with 3rd as it turns west, then south, away from North Avenue. At the stop sign turn east on Coombsville Road, then turn immediately south on 4th Avenue, which zigs and zags over three little rollers down to Imola Avenue East. Skyline Park located here can be an enjoyable picnic stop. Imola descends gradually and passes two roadside markets before crossing Highway 121 (Soscol Avenue) at mile **7.4**. Continue west and cross the green drawbridge over the Napa River, where a shopping center and plenty of services can be found on the west side. This is the most congested portion of the journey, but fortunately it ends as you cross under Highway 29.

Turn south on Golden Gate Drive toward the Napa C.H.P. office. Golden Gate becomes a frontage for Highway 29 and ends with a south turn into a stand of eucalyptus trees that line Stanley Lane. Turn west onto the wide shoulder of Highway 121/12 and begin to ascend a gradual hill, with grapes as far as you can see. At the crest, turn north on Old Sonoma Road (no sign), where a small market (closed Sundays) is just off the highway. Stay on Old Sonoma through the next turn north and continue through vineyards for just over a mile before turning north again on Buhman Avenue. Climb a little hill and descend past houses to a stop sign at Browns Valley Road. Take Browns Valley northwest, then turn west onto Redwood Road at mile **17.3**. Redwood Road climbs and drops in the cool shade, passes houses nestled in the trees, and travels alongside Redwood Creek up to Mt.Veeder Road. Now comes the fun part. Don't let the profile scare you; this is a very enjoyable climb with a nice 8.2% pitch before the summit to get the heart pumping.

Those big numbers painted on the street are addresses so emergency vehicles can quickly locate any house in these hills: smart idea. The summit at Lokoya Road is followed by a beautiful descent that presents one fantastic vista after another. The drop to Dry Creek

Highway 128 (in Lower Chiles Valley)

Road is very fast, so take it easy your first time down. Turn east on Dry Creek and drop just a little more before veering north away from Dry Creek Road to climb the backside of Oakville Grade. The climb to the summit at mile **30.1** is short, but the views of the Napa Valley spread out below seem to go on forever.

The descent on Oakville Grade is very steep. Take it easy here. After a mile of flat land at the bottom turn south on busy Highway 29 and continue another mile to Yount Mill Road, then go east. Yount Mill will take you to the outskirts of Yountville; services can be found here if you need them. Take Yountville Cross Road east through the vineyards to Silverado Trail at mile **37.3**, then go south. Silverado is wide, gradual, and busy; I prefer narrow, steep, and lonely Mt. Veeder Road. Stay with Silverado 6.7 miles, past a golf course (water and restrooms) to Hardman Avenue. Turn east and climb, then drop to Atlas Peak Road in front of the Silverado Country Club. Atlas Peak takes you south to Monticello Road where the grocery at Vichy Avenue is in sight.

20 THE ATLAS ASCENT _____

Starting Point: *Napa*
Distance: *20.6 miles up & down*
Total Climb: *2,160 ft.*

Average Pavement Quality: *1.7*
Map: *Pages 60-61*

Here's a nice short ride for all you hill climbers and mountain persons. With 104 feet per mile, Atlas Peak Road has more gain per mile than any other route in this book. The climb, although long, is never steeper than 8% and averages just over 4%. On the way up, there are fantastic views to the northeast and into the southern Napa Valley as well. The southern portion of the mountain is dotted with houses, which continue to spring up, even though the area was burned a few years ago. The middle part of the climb is open land with oaks, pines, and manzanita scrub. The upper portion is tree-shaded, with a vineyard tucked into a small valley. A lone house a half mile before the locked gate has a water faucet near the street. The summit of Atlas Peak is over 2,660 feet, but the road above the 2,050-foot elevation is private property and inaccessible. Because there is no place to go but down from the gate, I have included the return distance in the trip's total. As you descend, some of the corners are sharp, but you will know where they are, having just climbed up them.

Begin at Val's Grocery on Monticello Road at Vichy where ROUTE #19 also begins. Be sure to have plenty of water for the nine-mile climb to come. Go southwest on Monticello for just a stone's throw to Atlas Peak Road and turn northwest. The Silverado Country Club is the focus for many of the fancy homes here in the lower hills. Begin the climb via some switchbacks, and pass a pet cemetery at mile **3.4**. After another mile of climbing, the road flattens as it passes a closed area surrounding the Milliken Reservoir watershed. Climb a short 5% section, then drop into a small valley where the Circle "S" Ranch raises cattle. More switchbacks at mile **8.1** signal the start of the steepest section at 7.9%. Stately old oaks guard the road and shade all passersby. The Sutro Ranch owns the property beyond the gate. There is not much of a view from here, but all the trees make a cool, shady place to rest before you turn around. The descent does have some tight corners and narrow spots, but take it easy and you should have no problems. Once you're back down past the Silverado Country Club, turn northeast on Monticello Road; the store you started from is just ahead.

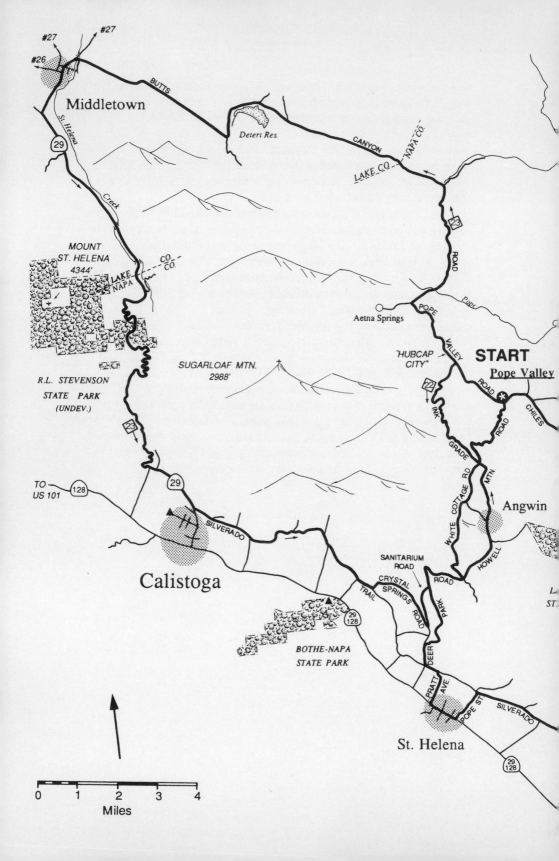

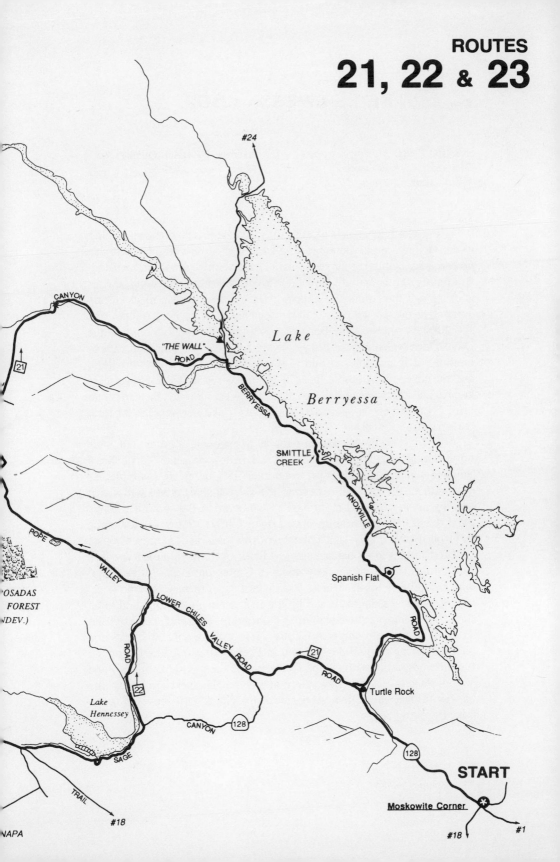

#24

CANYON

"THE WALL"
ROAD

21

BERRYESSA

Lake

Berryessa

SMITTLE
CREEK

KNOXVILLE

POPE

VALLEY

OSADAS
FOREST
(NDEV.)

Spanish Flat

LOWER CHILES VALLEY ROAD

21

ROAD

ROAD

Turtle Rock

22

Lake
Hennessey

CANYON

128

SAGE

128

TRAIL

START

#18

NAPA

#18

#1

Moskowite Corner

21 LAKE BERRYESSA LOOP _____

Starting Point: *Moskowite Corner*
Distance: *45.1 mile loop*
Total Climb: *1,710 ft.*

Average Pavement Quality: *1.3*
Map: *Pages 68-69*

     Lake Berryessa is a gem. But because it is so popular, cycling in the vicinity on busy summer weekends can be downright crazy. It's no fun being a moving target for some nerd with an empty in his hand. But during spring and fall the lake is quiet, the roads are empty, the air is crisp, and the colors are fantastic. This ride is within reach of any competent cyclist who can handle occasional wide boat trailers and shoulderless roads. Lake Berryessa is a favorite of mine because the Davis Double Century has nearly always traveled its shores and valleys on those early mornings of mid-May. Food and water are no problem, as there are enough of those "beer-bait-deli-ice-snacks-video-eat-get-gas-laundromat-marina-pizza" places along the west shore to take care of an army. Avoid busy summer weekends, and Lake Berryessa is a nearly perfect place to cycle.
     Start from the parking lot at Moskowite Corner and head northeast on wide Highway 128. At **4.8** miles, pass the Turtle Rock Store to which you will return in another 35.5 miles after completing your tour of the lake. Just beyond the store a short climb will warm you up quickly on cool mornings. A vineyard at the summit extends clear down to the turn north onto Lower Chiles Valley Road at mile **7.9** (pronounced Chy-els). Watch for this turn, as it is easy to miss. Lower Chiles Valley has a vineyard from one end to the other. The road climbs and drops abruptly down to Chiles and Pope Valley Road, which continues north. Chiles Valley is a superior place to ride year-round; wide, smooth roads and light traffic seem almost too good to be true. A picturesque stone wall lines the road for a short distance at mile **12.2.** Descend into northern Chiles Valley where an easy climb and another short drop will deposit you in Pope Valley. At the bottom of the hill veer northeast on Pope Canyon Road and pass the quiet Pope Valley Airport. Leave the valley at the gravel operation, cross the narrow bridge, and follow alongside Pope Creek as it seeks refuge in Lake Berryessa below.

Highway 128 (at Lower Chiles Valley Road)

The summit of "The Wall" provides a panoramic first view of the lake. After the quick 7.2% drop, turn south on Berryessa Knoxville Road and cross the graffiti-covered bridge at mile **27.4**. There are few signs of civilization visible from the road, especially in this northern section. Smittle Creek picnic area has water, restrooms, and shady areas overlooking the lake. Pass the new Bureau of Reclamation Visitor Information Center at mile **33.7**. Leave the lakeshore for the last time at Capell Cove and climb gradually back up to Turtle Rock Store on Highway 128. It is another 4.8 easy miles south back to Moskowite Corner.

22 NAPA & CHILES VALLEY TOUR

Starting Point: *Pope Valley*
Distance: *36.1 mile loop*
Total Climb: *2,190 ft.*

Average Pavement Quality: *1.2*
Map: *Pages 68-69*

I will never forget the first time I rode up to Angwin via Ink Grade. It was a warm summer day, but the road was so nicely shaded I didn't notice the heat. As the road climbed, the air became cooler and a breeze whispered through the pines. In such beautiful surroundings, physical discomforts seem to disappear. Howell Mountain is just such a place; even though the climb is formidable, it doesn't seem that strenuous.

After an exhilarating plunge down the mountain, the shady park on Main Street in St. Helena (pronounced Hell-ee-na) is a great place to relax. There are many food and drink options in town; the market near the park is a good choice. This route also contains another of my all time favorite roads: the Chiles and Pope Valley Road above Lake Hennessey. Enough said. This is a good ride.

The journey begins from the H&M Market in Pope Valley (open 10 am to 7 pm, seven days). Take Pope Valley Road northwest

1.7 miles, turn west, and begin the pleasant climb up Ink Grade. The steepest section (7.5%) begins two miles later where you pass a cozy house with a palm tree near the road. The forest changes from oaks to pines as you ascend. When you reach White Cottage Road, turn south (right). Climb just a bit more before dropping down to the stop sign at College Avenue. Angwin is a short side trip to the south. To continue, climb again on White Cottage Road and at mile **7.4** prepare for six miles of grand descent. The only tricky spot is the turn west onto Deer Park Road, where there is a stop sign at the bottom of a fast 7.7% pitch. All the other corners are well marked in advance. At the bottom, turn south on Silverado Trail, travel just over a half mile, then turn west onto Pratt Avenue on the stone bridge. Turn southeast on Main Street (Highway 29/128) and head into St. Helena.

There is plenty to see, do, and eat, so plan to spend some time here. Continue south on Main Street. A nice bike shop can be found just before the turn northeast onto Pope Street at mile **15.8**. At the east end of Pope, take Silverado Trail southeast 3.3 miles to Sage Canyon Road (Highway 128) and head east to Conn Dam. At the far end of Lake Hennessey, turn north on the newly paved Chiles and Pope

Ink Grade (above Pope Valley)

Valley Road. The climb begins when you cross the old bridge at mile 25.1. The road levels out where Lower Chiles Valley Road intersects, above the site of the Chiles Grist Mill (built in 1845). You are now entering vineyard-filled Chiles Valley, where the road provides marvelous vistas. Continue northwest on Chiles and Pope Valley. Only one little hill at mile 33.5 remains before you drop into Pope Valley and finish at the H&M Market where you began. Hey, that was only thirty-six miles; we could do that again!

23 ANGWIN ANGWISH

Starting Point: *Pope Valley*
Distance: *52.2 mile loop*
Total Climb: *3,710 ft.*

Average Pavement Quality: *1.3*
Map: *Pages 68-69*

This is a challenging half-century, with terrain varying widely from oak-dotted hills to open scrub, from high pine forest to low fertile valley. There is also a sizable amount of climbing plus two of the most radical descents in this book. The 5.9-mile plunge down Highway 29 into Calistoga should not be attempted if you are at all squeamish about sharing a shoulderless hairpin corner with a forty-foot semi and a camper pulling a boat. The climb past the sanitarium to Angwin is a steep little hill, but the real fun begins when your brakes overheat on the 9.6% drop into Pope Valley. Hey, you'll love it!

From Pope Valley's H&M Market (open 10 am to 7 pm, seven days), head northwest on Pope Valley Road, being sure to say "Hi" to Litto, the old man at "Hubcap City." The road changes its name to Butts Canyon Road at Aetna Springs Road, swings east, crosses a new bridge, and begins to climb at mile 5.1. This next portion was recently paved, which makes the descent much nicer and safer than it used to be. Pass Snell Valley Road and climb again, gradually at first, crossing into Lake County at mile 8.7. Crest out into a vineyard-filled valley, which gets its water from Detert Reservoir up ahead. Beyond the reservoir, ascend into another valley and roll into Middletown for a well-deserved break. There are plenty of food options such as a grocery, a pizza place, and my favorite--a small deli on the far end of town. The Lake County portion of Highway 29 from Middletown is wide and gradual to the Napa County line where the shoulder disappears and the climb steepens. A roadside spring a half mile farther is a perfect place to fill your bottles and regroup for the next 2.7 miles to the summit.

There is a passing lane for most of the ascent, but be extra alert because you are hard to see in the curvy, shady stretches of this northern side of Mt. St. Helena. The 2,250-foot summit is the highest point on any Napa County route. Be advised that this white-knuckle screamer has the largest, most sustained drop of any route in any of the four counties. Once safely to the bottom, continue south by turning onto Silverado Trail at mile **35.6**, just past a fruit stand. The stores and mud baths of Calistoga are only a half mile off to the west. Roll along through the grapes for 5.8 miles, then turn east on Crystal Springs Road and climb up into a small valley with more vineyards. (This is a pleasant shortcut to avoid the narrow climb on lower Deer Park Road.) Gear down for the 9.5% grade as you turn north on Sanitarium Road at the stop sign. Just beyond the crest turn north again on Deer Park Road and keep on crankin'. Continue straight, now on Howell Mountain Road at mile **46.3**, with 1.7 miles of cool forest before Angwin.

Pacific Union College is Angwin, surrounded by nice homes tucked into the forest. The stores and gas station are closed on Saturday, in keeping with Adventist church policy. Two miles of easy climbing in the pines are all that stand between you and "the drop!" It isn't long, but it is steep: one section at 10% to be exact, although it seems steeper. A series of tight corners and switchbacks forces you to stay on the brakes all the way to Pope Valley below. As quickly as it began, it's over, with your car waiting patiently across the street, beside the store.

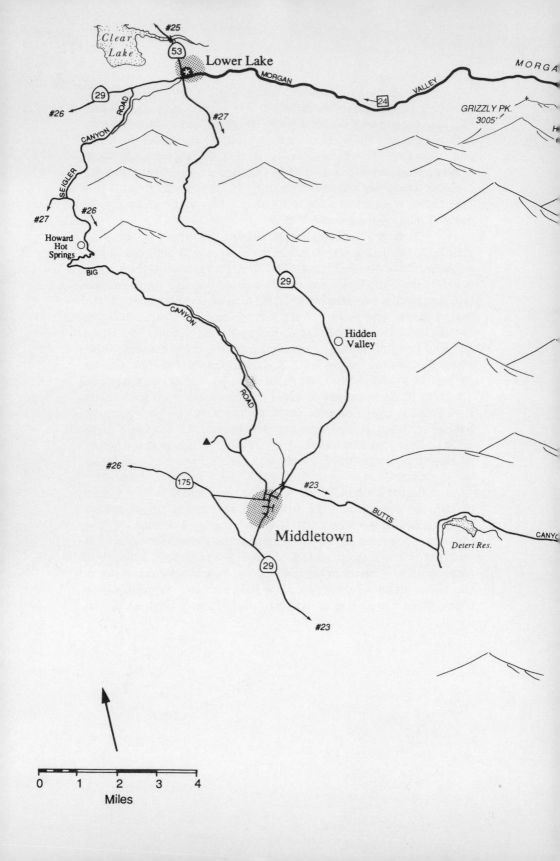

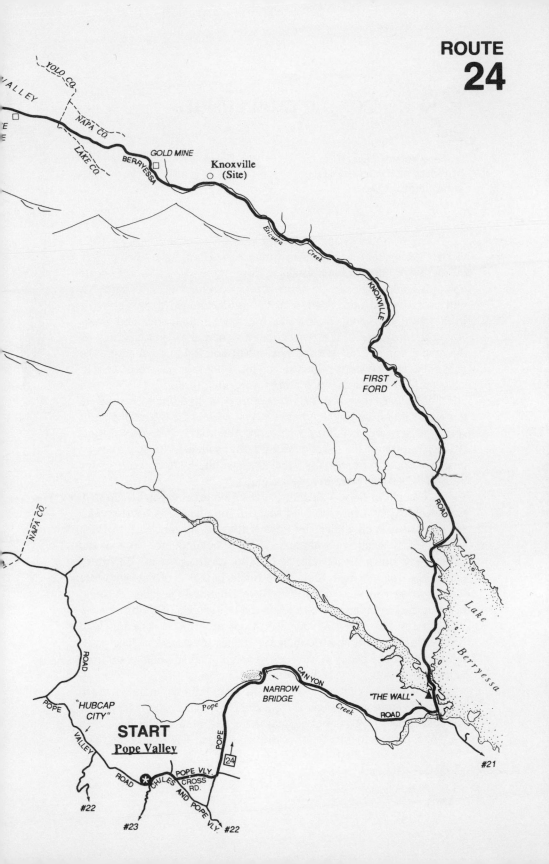

YOLO CO.

VALLEY

NAPA CO.

LAKE CO.

BERRYESSA

GOLD MINE

Knoxville
(Site)

Bticuera

Creek

KNOXVILLE

FIRST
FORD

NAPA CO.

ROAD

Lake
Berryessa

CAN YON

NARROW
BRIDGE

Pope

Creek

ROAD

"THE WALL"

"HUBCAP
CITY"

ROAD

POPE

START
Pope Valley

VALLEY

POPE

24

#21

POPE VLY.
CROSS
RD.

CHILES

AND

POPE VLY.

#22

ROAD

#22

#23

24 KNOXVILLE CHALLENGE _____

Starting Point: *Pope Valley*
Distance: *47.7 miles one way*
Total Climb: *3,080 ft.*

Average Pavement Quality: *1.7*
Map: *Pages 76-77*

This route is the rough-cut jewel of Napa County. I rediscovered this route in my curiosity about the Homestake Mine project on the Napa-Lake County border. Homestake Mine is a large-scale open-pit gold mine operated under strict environmental safeguards. It will be converted into a park after the gold is mined out. Knoxville itself was once a gold-mining site, but stone foundations and grass-covered tailings are all that remain today. The Lake County portion of the road (Morgan Valley Road) was mostly dirt and gravel before the project began. Now it is wide and smooth Grade One pavement clear to Lower Lake, with some nice climbs and one big descent. The road north of Lake Berryessa crisscrosses a creek twelve times on concrete low-water fords; so be careful after heavy rains in the winter and early spring. There are very few people along this route. All you will find are a few cows grazing among the oaks, and solitude. Be sure to carry plenty of food and especially water because there are no services for 37.2 miles between Lake Berryessa and Clear Lake.

Begin in Pope Valley at the H&M Market (open 10 am to 7 pm, seven days). Bring food and water if you plan to start earlier than 10 am. Go east on Chiles and Pope Valley Road, turn east on Pope Valley Cross Road, then north on Pope Canyon Road. Follow the little creek down to the lake and turn north again on Berryessa Knoxville Road at mile **10.3.** Five miles farther is a lone outhouse with a wonderful view down the entire length of the lake. A small ranch at the beginning of the valley is the last vestige of civilization for many miles. The first of the fords is at mile **20.3.** The last is at Knoxville. If there is more than six inches of water or slick green moss, it would be better to walk across them. Fall is a marvelous time in the canyon--cool, dry, and colorful.

There isn't much happening in Knoxville anymore. In fact, the only greeting you will get is from the noisy cattle guard there. The steepest climb (7.6%) is just beyond the Knoxville Devilhead Road (a B.L.M. access road) with the shot-to-pieces sign. The first of the mine project buildings is after the climb at mile **30.5**, where a tunnel allows the heavy earthmovers to pass overhead. I have ridden here midweek and on weekends, but the trucks and the digging operation are almost invisible from the road. The only signs of anything out of place are the few buildings and the well-manicured roadcut. The views in all directions are fantastic. The terrain is hilly and rolling, mostly brush, short grass, and oak-dotted valleys with scattered stands of digger pines.

The highest point (2,500') is marked by the first of three "trucks use low gear" signs at mile **37.5**. The second sign is at the start of the long descent, with the steep section beginning at the third sign. The mining area ends at a short climb. Descend into another little valley with scattered houses and continue to Lower Lake. There is a good market there (open 9 am to 6 pm, seven days) and a cafe around the corner, on Highway 53.

There are several ways to get back to Pope Valley. My favorite is climbing Seigler Canyon Road and descending Big Canyon Road to Middletown (see ROUTES #27 and #26), and taking Butts Canyon Road (see ROUTE #23) from there. To get back quickly, take Highway 29 to Middletown, and Butts Canyon from there; this adds only 32.5 miles for a round-trip of 80.2 miles.

LAKE COUNTY

LAKE COUNTY
INTRODUCTION _____

Lake County can be divided into two regions: the northern, with very few paved roads or habitations, and the southern, with the recreational attractions of Clear Lake and the Cobb Mountain resort area. The northern area, while fantastic for fat-tire exploration, loses most of its appeal for bikes with skinny tires. I will therefore cover only the paved, hilly southern part of the county.

The Cobb Mountain area is a fantastic place to cycle, but not for the novice, I'm afraid. Most of the roads are narrow and can be long, steep undertakings, with the few that are wide usually carrying fast traffic. Clear Lake, on the other hand, is a wonderful place for riders of all abilities who enjoy traveling through miles of quiet pear orchards and walnut groves while taking in beautiful vistas of the lake.

Lakeport, on the western shore of Clear Lake, is the largest town in the county, but still falls well within the small town catagory. This and most of the other towns that line the shore are based largely on agriculture and also on the summer tourist industry, which has seen better days. Many retirees now choose to make their homes around Clear Lake and in the communities that dot the surrounding mountains and valleys. Near the southwestern border of the county, the small towns of Kelseyville and Middletown have experienced some recent growth and prosperity because of geothermal development. Both Cobb Mountain routes (ROUTES #26 and #27) begin in Middletown to take advantage of the services there, but other starting points are always possible. A great asset of this area are the numerous small resort communities, which make ideal rest and refueling spots. Add to that the feeling of being off in the mountains, miles from anywhere, and you can understand why this area is a favorite of the few cyclists who have discovered it.

Wind, typically blowing out of the northwest, can affect the ride around Clear Lake. Almost all the mountain roads are protected from wind by the trees, but it can get chilly at 3,000 feet, even in the summer. Snow does fall a couple times each winter in the Cobb Mountain area. Winter rain totals are almost twice that of Davis. You can also expect summer temperatures in Lakeport and the valleys near Middletown to be higher than in Davis (which is known for its heat). It gets hot in the mountains too, but the shade and breezes take some of the edge off it.

The miles of narrow, twisting, often steep roads can be hazardous for two reasons: increased downhill speeds and decreased sight distances. Also, local traffic moves quickly along familiar roads, not expecting to see cyclists. So stay alert and take it easy, especially your first time through.

Although the total mileage of cycling roads in Lake County is fairly small, even the most well-traveled cyclist will find abundant beauty and ample challenge here. Good things often come in small packages. So, enjoy.

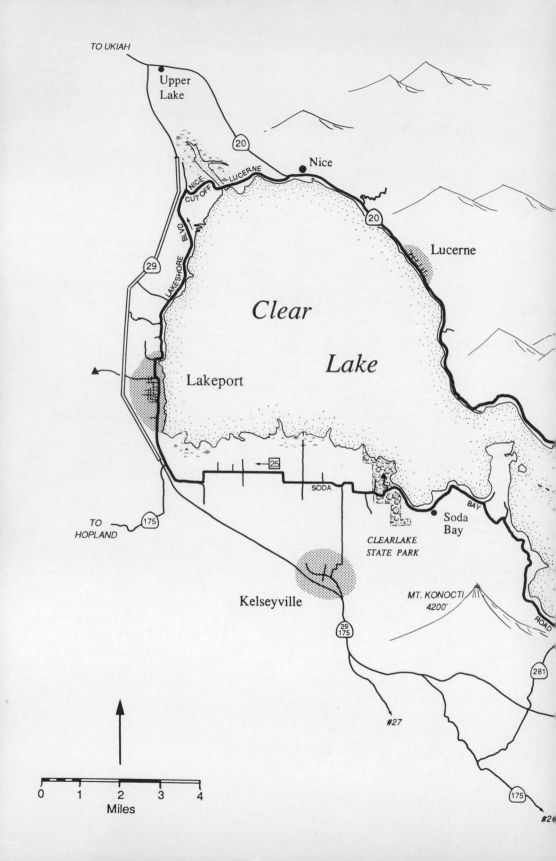

TO UKIAH

Upper
Lake

20

NICE—LUCERNE CUT OFF

LAKESHORE BLVD

Nice

20

Lucerne

29

Clear

Lake

Lakeport

25

SODA

TO
HOPLAND

175

CLEARLAKE
STATE PARK

Soda
Bay

BAY

Kelseyville

29
175

MT. KONOCTI
4200'

ROAD

281

#27

0   1   2   3   4

Miles

175

#2

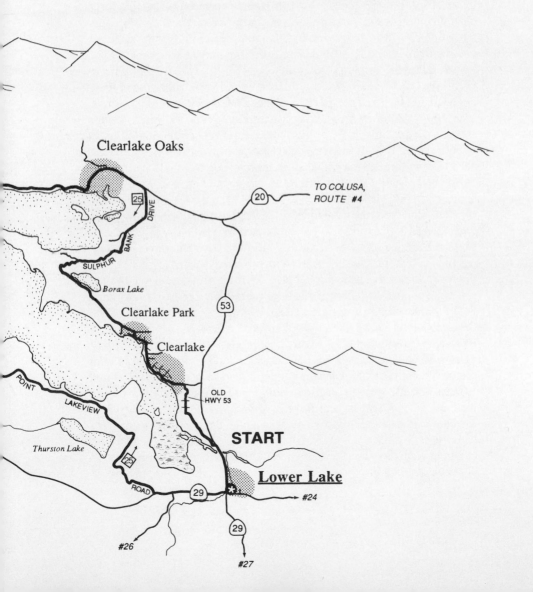

Clearlake Oaks

TO COLUSA,
ROUTE #4

20

25

DRIVE

BANK

SULPHUR

Borax Lake

53

Clearlake Park

Clearlake

POINT

LAKEVIEW

OLD
HWY 53

Thurston Lake

25

START

ROAD

29

Lower Lake

#24

29

#26

#27

25 CLEAR AROUND CLEAR LAKE _____

Starting Point: *Lower Lake*
Distance: *62.8 mile loop*
Total Climb: *2,230 ft.*

Average Pavement Quality: *1.8*
Map: *Pages 84-85*

Did you know that Clear Lake is the largest natural lake completely within California? That helps to explains why this is the longest route of the book. The trip takes you through continuously changing terrain and views of the very pretty lake. As with any water attraction in California, however, the summer months can be rather crowded with tourists. One way to avoid the masses would be to ride just to Lakeport and back, skipping busy Highway 20 from Nice to Clearlake Oaks. The fall is the finest time, however, after the crowds have left and the trees are on fire with color. Lake County is a volcanic area, as evidenced by the striking Mount Konocti on the southwestern shore of Clear Lake and the mineral deposits at Sulphur Bank on the eastern shore. Lake County produces red pumice rock, which has been used to pave some of the roads with an interesting effect. If you choose to ride in the spring and fall, this route can provide an enjoyable tour of a unique natural wonder.

Start from the little town of Lower Lake and take Highway 29 west toward Kelseyville. A half mile past Seigler Canyon Road turn north on Point Lakeview Road. You will notice the pavement is a unique shade of red, having been paved with rock from a quarry just up the road. Past the quarry is a fun little drop and a climb back up to the same elevation, followed by a much longer and steeper drop to near lake level. At the next summit are houses, a golf course, and some of the best panoramic views of the southern lake. Turn north on Soda Bay Road at mile **8.9**; there is a small shopping area to the left. Soda Bay Road travels through a beautiful, dense fir forest with ferns and cool moss-covered rocks that have tumbled from the north side of Mount Konocti. Turn west to continue along Soda Bay Road at a poorly marked "T" intersection and head into the quiet village of Soda Bay. McDaniels Market at mile **15.7** is open seven days a week, from 9 am to at least 5 pm. Clear Lake State Park is 1.8 miles ahead, with camping and day use facilities. A half mile farther, turn west to continue on Soda Bay Road. The road is now flat as you travel through some of Lake County's famous pear orchards, on the way to Lakeport at mile **25.0**.

The only place I have ever eaten in Lakeport is the Cottage Coffee Shop, on the right about a mile past the big grocery store. For a good price, they serve a plate full of pancakes, eggs, and sausages on outdoor tables. Lakeport has a park and other food possibilities, if this is your turn-around point. To continue, stay on Main Street through Lakeport another 0.1 mile, then jog west on Clearlake Avenue, go north on High Street, and finally return to the shore of the lake on Lakeshore Boulevard. Take the Nice-Lucerne Cutoff east, across a low bridge, and over to Nice and Highway 20. There is a shoulder from here past Lucerne where the Foster's Freeze has classic 3-D pictures of a cat and a dog. Beyond Lucerne, the next services are in Clearlake Oaks at mile **49.1**. Turn south 1.8 miles past Clearlake Oaks on Sulphur Bank Drive and climb once again.

At the summit it looks as if there are two lakes, one to the north and one to the south, rather than just one lake seen from a peninsula. Drop down past Borax Lake and enter a residential area. Veer southeast on poorly marked Arrowhead Road. Then take the third turn south on Park Street, go about 400 feet, then turn south on Lakeshore. The city of Clearlake has seen brighter days, but things are looking better. There are plenty of services as you roll along the shore. Pass Redbud Park, which can be a nice post-ride picnic spot. At the stop light, turn south on Old Highway 53, which will take you down to (new) Highway 53. From here it is only 1.5 miles south to Lower Lake where you began.

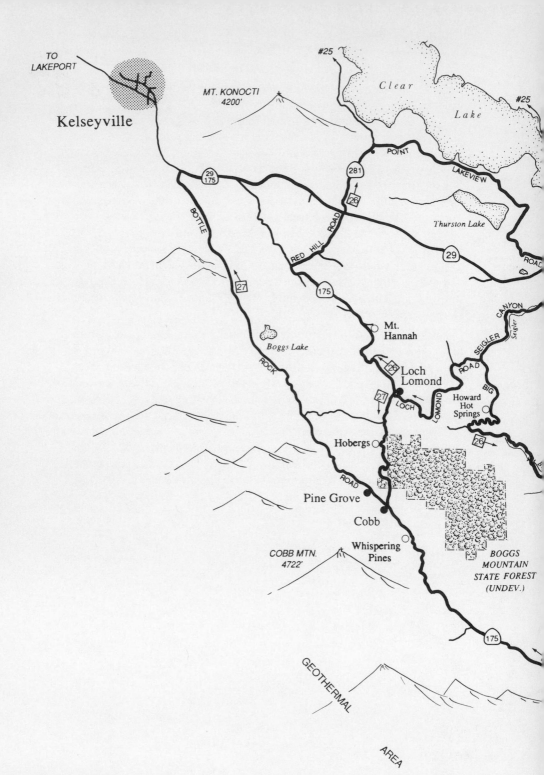

TO
LAKEPORT

Kelseyville

MT. KONOCTI
4200'

Clear
Lake

#25

#25

POINT

LAKEVIEW

29
175

281

26

Thurston Lake

29

ROAD

BOTTLE

RED HILL ROAD

175

27

ROCK

Boggs Lake

Mt.
Hannah

26

Loch
Lomond

27

LOCH

LOMOND

SEIGLER ROAD

CANYON

Seigler

BIG

Howard
Hot
Springs

26

Hobergs

ROAD

Pine Grove

Cobb

Whispering
Pines

COBB MTN.
4722'

BOGGS
MOUNTAIN
STATE FOREST
(UNDEV.)

175

GEOTHERMAL

AREA

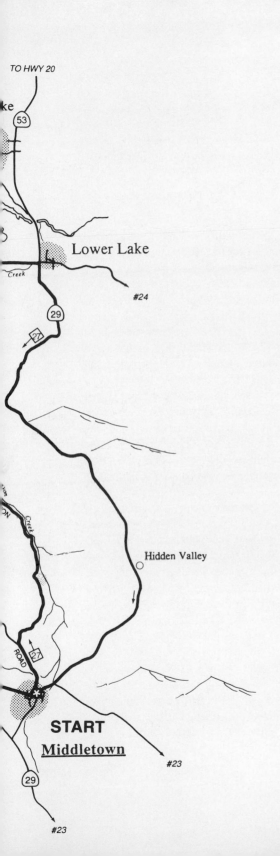

TO HWY 20

53

Lower Lake

Creek

#24

29

27

Hidden Valley

ROAD

27

START

Middletown

#23

29

#23

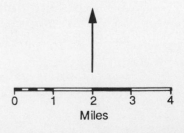

| 0 | 1 | 2 | 3 | 4 |

Miles

26 COBB MOUNTAIN CLIMB _____

Starting Point: *Middletown*
Distance: *45.4 mile loop*
Total Climb: *3,730 ft.*

Average Pavement Quality: *1.9*
Map: *Pages 84-85*

If you have been looking at the profiles, I'm sure you have noticed these last two routes and have commented on the rather large amount of climbing in a fairly short distance. Well, if you want hills, we got hills! This is not the place for the novice cyclist to try out new equipment. Many of the roads are steep, narrow, and curvy, with less than ideal sight distance on the tree-shaded roads. Fast traffic is also a factor on the miles of state highways. For you experienced riders, however, this area is an untapped resource, with some of the most beautiful and challenging roads you will ever find. The Cobb Mountain Climb can be ridden in either direction. Climbing up Highway 175 to Cobb is a tough little grunt, due to the steep, narrow road and warm southern exposure. But riding from Loch Lomond Resort down to Point Lakeview Road is a delightful cruise through fir, pine, and oak forests, through walnut orchards, and finally into open scrub. Seigler Canyon and Big Canyon are always fun no matter in which direction you travel. If you have never ridden here before or are looking for a new challenge, look no further.

From the Middletown High School parking lot, head south into town and turn west on Highway 175 toward Cobb Mountain. Begin to climb and pass Socrates Mine Road, where trucks travel to and from the geothermal power plant. Whispering Pines comes none too soon, with cool shade and easier climbing ahead. The resort town of Cobb has a gas station, a store, and a restaurant open seven days a week. Climb to Hobergs, the highest point in this guide at 3,025 feet, one of many summer home communities on Cobb Mountain. If you didn't already know it, you wouldn't believe this quiet little road is a state highway. Loch Lomond at mile **11.9** is the other community on Cobb Mountain with a store and a restaurant; it is at the upper end of Loch Lomond Road (see ROUTE #27). Continue to descend, passing occasional homes, through groves of tall pines that come right up to the road. Turn east on Red Hills Road, climb just a bit, then drop quickly down to Highway 29 at mile **19.1**. After the stop sign,

Big Canyon Road (near Howard Hot Springs)

continue ahead; this section of road is labeled Highway 281. Slow down as you approach a small shopping center, and just beyond it, turn east on Point Lakeview Road. Pass by homes surrounded by a golf course. Then prepare to drop rather abruptly and climb back even more abruptly at 9.1%. The red pumice pavement begins at the crest and continues clear down to Highway 29 at mile **28.0**. Turn east here, being alert for fast traffic in both directions. After a half mile, turn south on Seigler Canyon Road. Climb alongside a pleasant creek that leads you up to the Loch Lomond Road-Big Canyon Road intersection.

If you feel like a pleasant 9.9% climb, give Loch Lomond Road a try. Some other time, maybe? Well then, take Big Canyon Road south. Just beyond the defunct resort of Howard Hot Springs, crest out, and then drop quickly as the road winds along the cliff. Watch for geese in the road as you sail past some secluded homes nestled into the canyon. The road parallels another small creek and crosses a narrow old white bridge at mile **37.6**. Continue the gradual descent past a small gravel operation, where the cool, shady canyon gives way to dry, open country, perfect for the grazing cattle. At the crest of a small hill veer south and drop into the valley. After crossing a creek, turn east on Wardlaw Street. The Middletown High School is just ahead.

27 LOCH LOMOND MONSTER _____

Starting Point: *Middletown*
Distance: *57.5 mile loop*
Total Climb: *3,500 ft.*

Average Pavement Quality: *1.5*
Map: *Pages 88-89*

This route is a mixed bag. Highway 29 can be busy and narrow, particularly near Kelseyville, but the terrain is interesting and the descents are fast and enjoyable. Loch Lomond Road was used in the 1984 Davis Double Century and caught almost everybody by surprise with a 10% climb in the warm May sun. Descending Cobb Mountain via Bottle Rock Road is another one of those white-knuckle screamers with a 7.6% average drop and a long pitch near the bottom at over 9.7%. However, the Cobb Mountain region with plenty of services is a fantastic cycling area and is made even more satisfying by the investment required to attain it. No matter which route you use, Big Canyon, Highway 175, Red Hills, Loch Lomond, or Bottle Rock--each is a worthy undertaking and will yield spectacular returns on your investment.

Before you start from Middletown High School, be sure to fill your water bottles because there are no services for the first seventeen miles. Head west on Wardlaw Street, then north on Big Canyon Road (the sign says Barnes Street). A short hill warms your legs as you leave the valley. Big Canyon is a pleasant and gradual climb, passing first through oaks and madrones, then pines and firs. Pass a small enclave of houses in the upper end of the valley, which is absolutely beautiful in the spring and fall. The exposed 6.3% climb out of the canyon is only 1.2 miles long, with fantastic views to the south. Beyond the crest, a hanging valley with a small airport marks your western turn onto Loch Lomond Road at mile **12.8**. Even though the first pitch is steep, the worst is over 1.2 miles ahead as the forest changes from oaks to firs and pines.

The feeling of accomplishment at reaching the summit is heightened by the feelings of joy and freedom up here on Cobb Mountain. The quiet Loch Lomond Resort lies 0.3 mile beyond the summit, where Loch Lomond Road ends at Highway 175. The store and restaurant are open from 8:30 am to 10 pm, seven days a week, and have restrooms around the back.

Turn south on smooth and shady Highway 175 and climb, then drop and climb again to the highest point in this guide, Hobergs. Descend quickly through some tight corners and continue to Cobb, where a gas station and a store (open seven days) can be found. Take Bottle Rock Road northwest at mile **20.2** and roll along through the cool forest and open valleys. Pine Grove has a small store and coffee shop open weekdays that caters to the geothermal power plant workers. After a nice smooth descent, the climb begins in earnest a half mile past Sulphur Creek Road. Bottle Rock Road is nearly straight, and you fly down the mountain and out into a vast brushy area south of Mount Konocti. Turn east on Highway 29/175. The next few miles have little, if any, shoulder, so be alert to other traffic. Highway 175 forks off to the south at mile **32.3** and can be an alternative to continuing on

Highway 175 (near Mt. Hannah)

to Lower Lake. Another challenging alternative, a little farther on, would be to take the north turn toward Soda Bay on Highway 281 and take Point Lakeview Road (see ROUTE #26).

Highway 29 rolls gradually through open country before dropping down nicely to Lower Lake at mile **43.1**. A long gradual climb followed by a fast drop through a small canyon will take you into Coyote Valley, with houses clustered around a small lake and golf course. Another easy ascent and drop, with occasional narrow spots, will take you back to Middletown, where you began.

APPENDICES

PROFILES

Profiles are a useful method of describing the topography of a route and showing distances between points. Here is an explanation of the format and symbols used.

* The vertical numbers refer to feet above mean sea level and the horizontal numbers refer to the distance in miles. The ratio of distance to elevation is 26.4:1.

* Labels are located at the center of a small feature (i.e. towns, landmarks, and road changes), or at the first contact with a larger feature (i.e.valleys, lakes, and cities).

* Shaded areas define climbs and drops steeper than 5.7% and longer than one-half mile. The percent figure with each gray tone is an average. There usually are steeper sections within each climb.

* The black dots indicate where services (food, etc.) can be found.

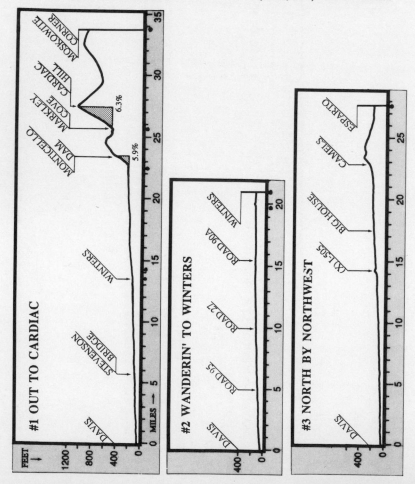

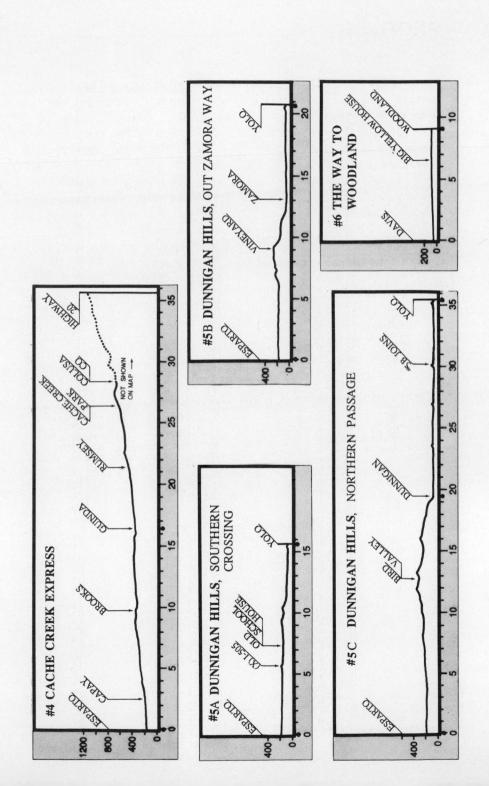

#4 CACHE CREEK EXPRESS

ESPARTO CAPAY BROOKS GUINDA RUMSEY CACHE CREEK PARK COLUSA CO HIGHWAY 20

NOT SHOWN ON MAP →

1200 800 400 0

0 5 10 15 20 25 30 35

#5A DUNNIGAN HILLS, SOUTHERN CROSSING

ESPARTO (XI-505) OLD SCHOOL HOUSE YOLO

400 0

0 5 10 15

#5B DUNNIGAN HILLS, OUT ZAMORA WAY

ESPARTO VINEYARD ZAMORA YOLO

400 0

5 10 15 20

#5C DUNNIGAN HILLS, NORTHERN PASSAGE

ESPARTO BIRD VALLEY DUNNIGAN 5B JOINS YOLO

400 0

0 5 10 15 20 25 30 35

#6 THE WAY TO WOODLAND

DAVIS BIG YELLOW HOUSE WOODLAND

200 0

0 5 10

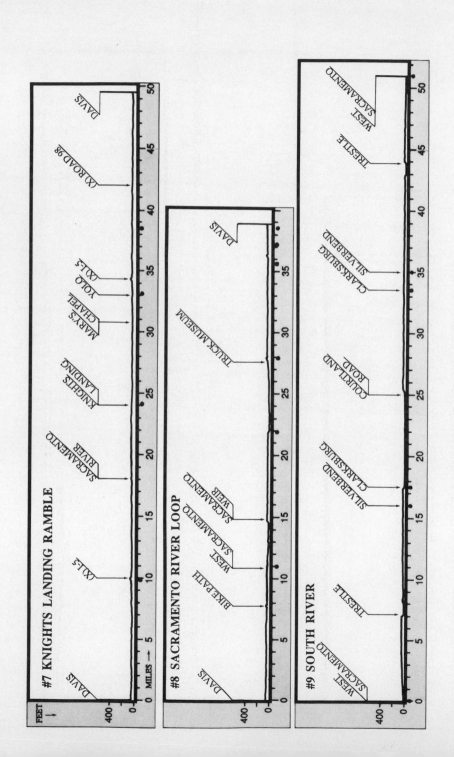

#7 KNIGHTS LANDING RAMBLE

DAVIS — (X) — KNIGHTS LANDING — SACRAMENTO RIVER — MARY'S CHAPEL — YOLO — (X) — (X) ROAD 98 — DAVIS

FEET — 400 — 0

#8 SACRAMENTO RIVER LOOP

DAVIS — BIKE PATH — WEST SACRAMENTO — SACRAMENTO WEIR — TRUCK MUSEUM — DAVIS

400 — 0

MILES — 0 5 10 15 20 25 30 35 40 45 50

#9 SOUTH RIVER

WEST SACRAMENTO — TRESTLE — SILVERBEND — CLARKSBURG — COURTLAND ROAD — CLARKSBURG — SILVERBEND — TRESTLE — WEST SACRAMENTO

400 — 0

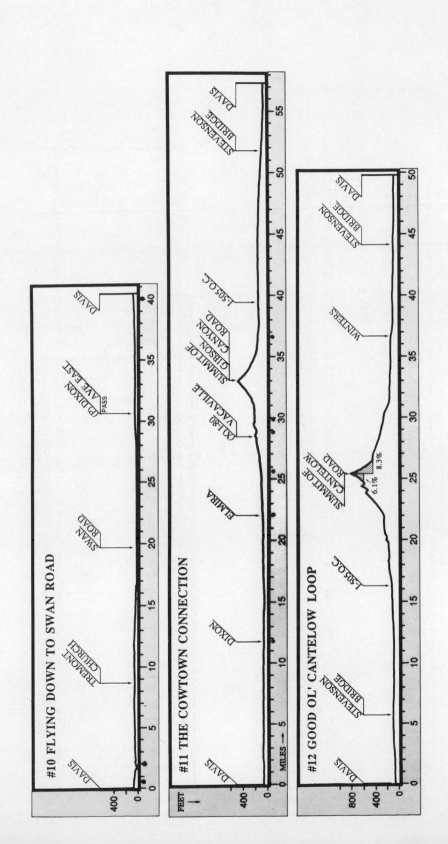

#10 FLYING DOWN TO SWAN ROAD

#11 THE COWTOWN CONNECTION

#12 GOOD OL' CANTELOW LOOP

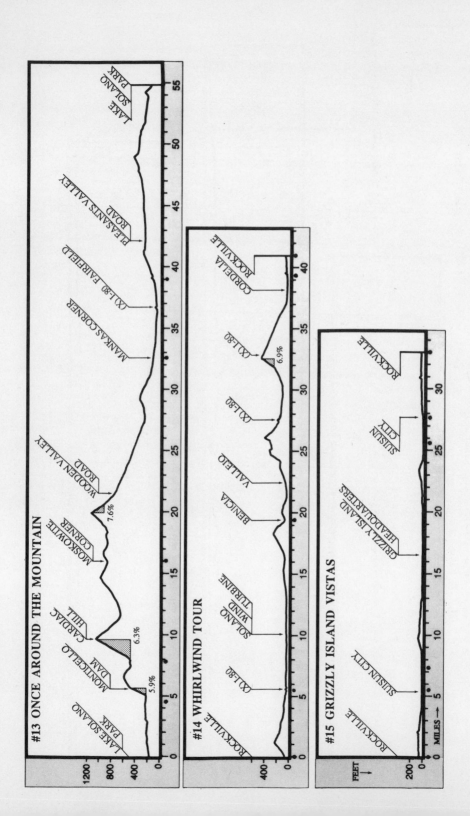

#13 ONCE AROUND THE MOUNTAIN

LAKE SOLANO PARK
MONTICELLO DAM
CARDIAC HILL
MOSKOWITE CORNER
WOODEN VALLEY ROAD
MANKA'S CORNER
(X) I-80 FAIRFIELD
PLEASANTS VALLEY ROAD
LAKE SOLANO PARK

5.9%
6.3%
7.6%

1200 800 400 0

#14 WHIRLWIND TOUR

ROCKVILLE
(X) I-80
SOLANO WIND TURBINE
BENICIA
VALLEJO
(X) I-80
(X) I-80
CORDELIA
ROCKVILLE

6.9%

400 0

#15 GRIZZLY ISLAND VISTAS

ROCKVILLE
SUISUN CITY
GRIZZLY ISLAND HEADQUARTERS
SUISUN CITY
ROCKVILLE

FEET →
200 0

MILES →

0   5   10   15   20   25   30   35   40   45   50   55

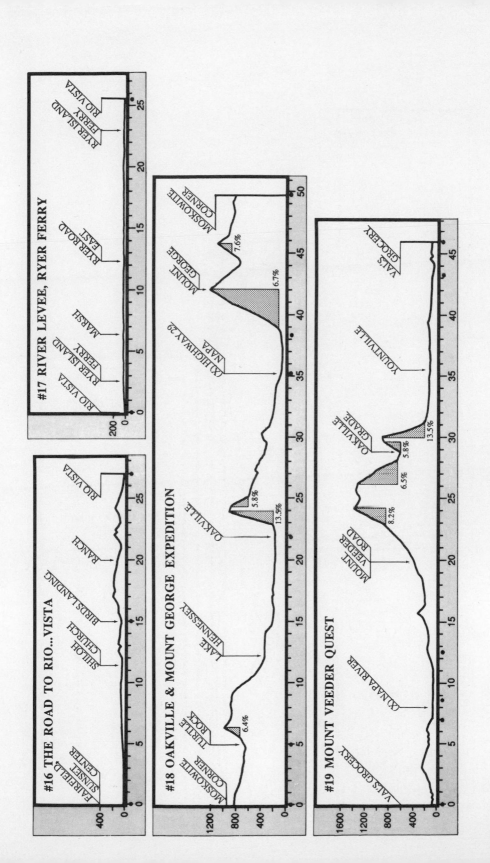

#16 THE ROAD TO RIO...VISTA

FAIRFIELD SUNSET CENTER
SHILOH CHURCH
BIRDSLANDING
RANCH
RIO VISTA

400
0

#17 RIVER LEVEE, RYER FERRY

RIO VISTA
RYER ISLAND FERRY
MARSH
RYER ROAD EAST
RYER ISLAND FERRY
RIO VISTA

200
0

0   5   10   15   20   25

#18 OAKVILLE & MOUNT GEORGE EXPEDITION

MOSKOWITE CORNER
TURTLE ROCK
6.4%
LAKE HENNESSEY
OAKVILLE
5.8%
13.5%
(X) HIGHWAY 29 NAPA
MOUNT GEORGE
6.7%
7.6%
MOSKOWITE CORNER

1200
800
400
0

0   5   10   15   20   25   30   35   40   45   50

#19 MOUNT VEEDER QUEST

VALS GROCERY
(X) NAPA RIVER
MOUNT VEEDER ROAD
8.2%
6.5%
OAKVILLE GRADE
5.8%
13.5%
YOUNTVILLE
VALS GROCERY

1600
1200
800
400
0

0   5   10   15   20   25   30   35   40   45

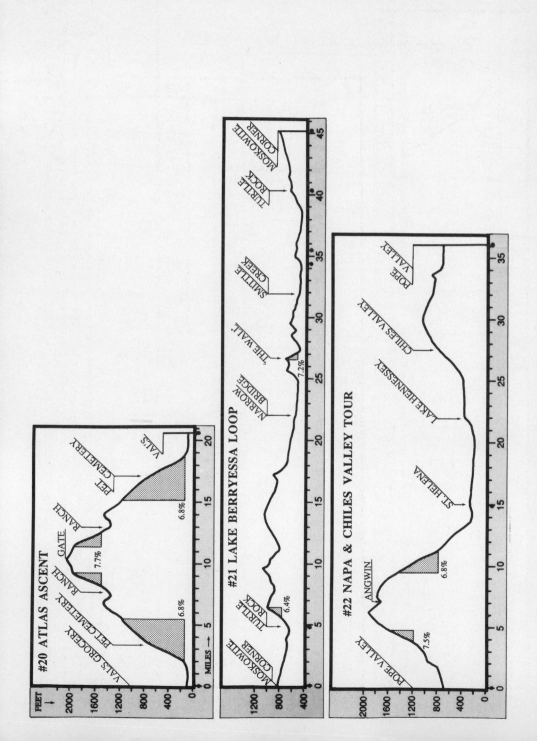

#20 ATLAS ASCENT

VALS GROCERY
PET CEMETERY
RANCH
GATE
RANCH
PET CEMETERY
VALS
6.8%
7.7%
6.8%

FEET
2000
1600
1200
800
400
0

MILES →
0   5   10   15   20

#21 LAKE BERRYESSA LOOP

MOSKOWITE CORNER
TURTLE ROCK
NARROW BRIDGE
'THE WALL'
SMITTLE CREEK
TURTLE ROCK
MOSKOWITE CORNER

6.4%
7.2%

1200
800
400

0   5   10   15   20   25   30   35   40   45

#22 NAPA & CHILES VALLEY TOUR

POPE VALLEY
ANGWIN
ST. HELENA
LAKE HENNESSEY
CHILES VALLEY
POPE VALLEY

7.5%
6.8%

2000
1600
1200
800
400
0

0   5   10   15   20   25   30   35

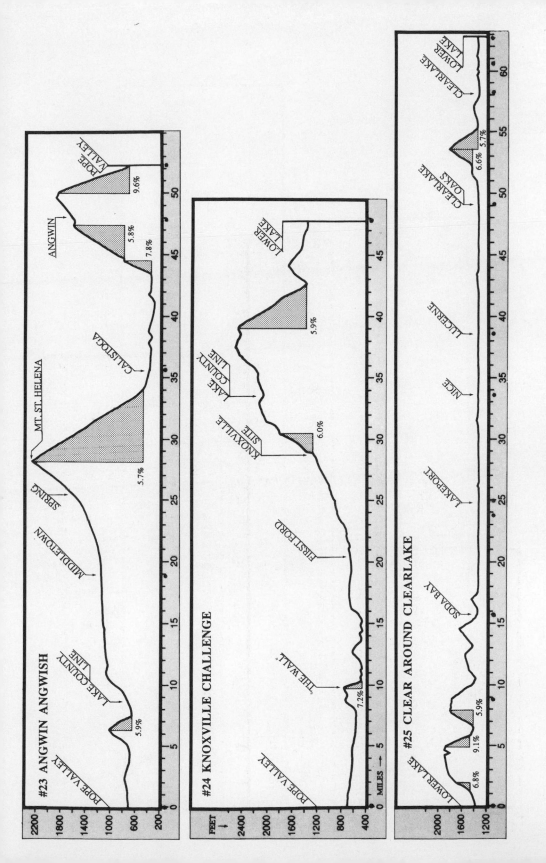

#23 ANGWIN ANGWISH

POPE VALLEY
LAKE COUNTY LINE
5.9%
MIDDLETOWN
SPRING
MT. ST. HELENA
5.7%
CALISTOGA
7.8%
ANGWIN
5.8%
9.6%
POPE VALLEY

2200 1800 1400 1000 600 200

#24 KNOXVILLE CHALLENGE

POPE VALLEY
"THE WALL"
7.2%
FIRST FORD
KNOXVILLE SITE
6.0%
LAKE COUNTY LINE
5.9%
LOWER LAKE

FEET

2400 2000 1600 1200 800 400

MILES ➞

#25 CLEAR AROUND CLEARLAKE

LOWER LAKE
6.8%
9.1%
5.9%
SODA BAY
LAKEPORT
NICE
LUCERNE
CLEARLAKE OAKS
6.6%
5.7%
CLEARLAKE
LOWER LAKE

2000 1600 1200

0 5 10 15 20 25 30 35 40 45 50 55 60

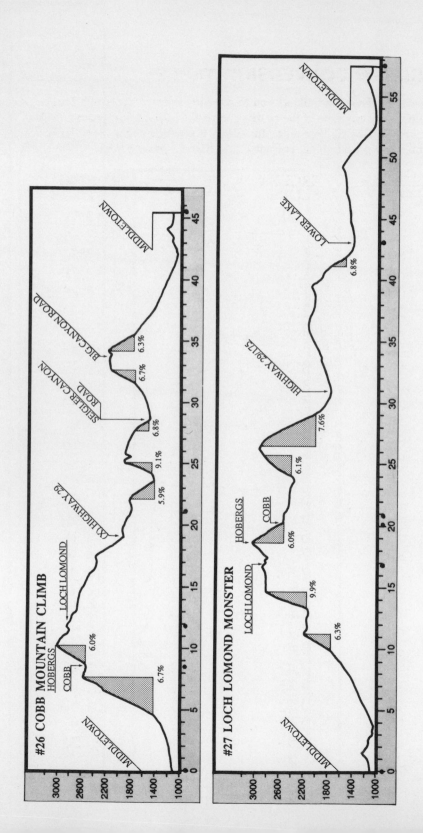

#26 COBB MOUNTAIN CLIMB

MIDDLETOWN
HOBERGS
COBB
LOCH LOMOND
(X) HIGHWAY 29
SEIGLER CANYON ROAD
BIG CANYON ROAD
MIDDLETOWN

6.0%
6.7%
5.9%
9.1%
6.8%
6.7%
6.3%

#27 LOCH LOMOND MONSTER

MIDDLETOWN
LOCH LOMOND
HOBERGS
COBB
HIGHWAY 29/175
LOWER LAKE
MIDDLETOWN

6.3%
9.9%
6.0%
6.1%
7.6%
6.8%

SLOPE CONVERSION TABLE _____

This chart allows you to correlate percent slope with feet per mile. For example, if the profile shows a climb at 6.8%, you would be climbing 360 feet per mile. Inversely, if you know how many feet per mile you are climbing, you can easily find the percent slope.

FEET PER MILE	PERCENT SLOPE	FEET PER MILE	PERCENT SLOPE
20	.38	20	11.74
40	.76	40	12.12
60	1.14	60	12.50
80	1.52	80	12.88
100	1.89	700	13.26
20	2.27	20	13.64
40	2.65	40	14.01
60	3.03	60	14.39
80	3.41	80	14.77
200	3.79	800	15.15
20	4.17	20	15.53
40	4.56	40	15.91
60	4.92	60	16.29
80	5.30	80	16.67
300	5.68	900	17.05
20	6.06	20	17.42
40	6.44	40	17.80
60	6.82	60	18.18
80	7.20	80	18.56
400	7.58	1000	18.94
20	7.95	20	19.32
40	8.33	40	19.70
60	8.71	60	20.08
80	9.09	80	20.45
500	9.47	1100	20.83
20	9.85	20	21.21
40	10.23	40	21.60
60	10.61	60	21.97
80	10.98	80	22.35
600	11.36	1200	22.73

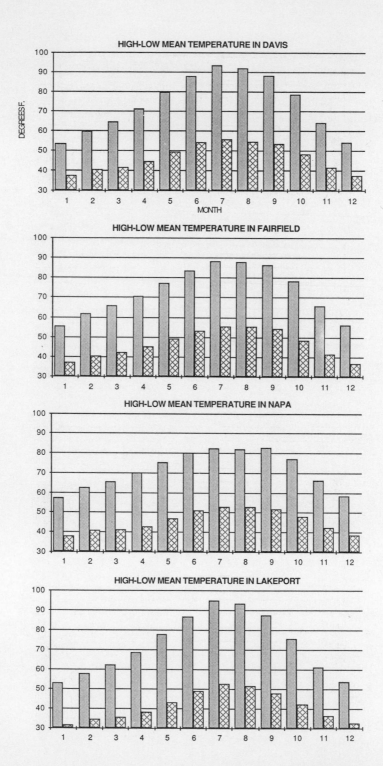

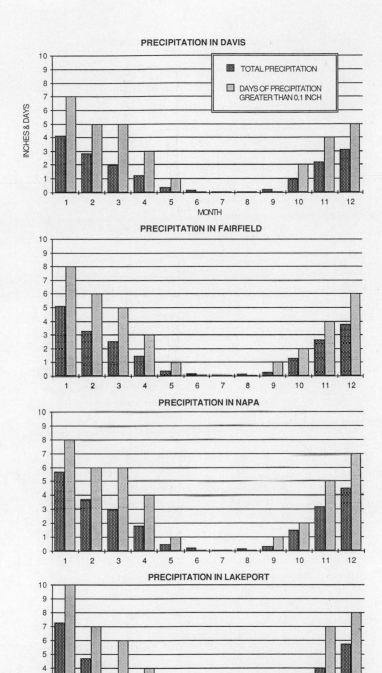

PAVEMENT QUALITY _____

This chart shows exactly how many miles of each pavement grade there are on each route.

ROUTE	GRADE ONE	GRADE TWO	GRADE THREE	GRADE FOUR	TOTAL MILES
#1	17.8	16.0	0	0	33.8
#2	6.7	14.3	0	0	21.0
#3	3.2	24.4	0	0	27.6
#4	0.9	27.4	0	0	28.3
#5 A	2.9	12.6	0	0	15.5
#5 B	4.2	13.9	2.5	0	20.6
#5 C	6.5	28.7	0	0	35.2
#6	5.1	4.0	0	0	9.1
#7	13.4	36.2	0	0	49.6
#8	22.5	15.3	0	0	38.8
#9	50.0	1.0	0	0	51.0
#10	36.9	3.5	0	0	40.4
#11	36.1	19.2	2.0	0	57.3
#12	18.2	28.3	3.2	<.02	49.7
#13	44.8	9.9	0	0	54.7
#14	22.6	11.9	6.4	0	40.9
#15	13.6	15.4	2.6	1.4	33.0
#16	12.6	14.3	0	0.1	27.0
#17	0.1	25.5	0	0	25.6
#18	32.5	17.1	0	0	49.6
#19	31.4	14.6	0	0	46.0
#20	6.8	13.8	0	0	20.6
#21	33.1	12.0	0	0	45.1
#22	28.4	7.7	0	0	36.1
#23	35.9	16.3	0	0	52.2
#24	14.7	31.4	1.6	0	47.7
#25	12.9	48.3	1.6	0	62.8
#26	5.2	38.6	1.6	0	45.4
#27	29.1	28.4	0	0	57.5